The European Union labour force survey
Methods and definitions

1996

Theme
Population and social conditions **3**
Series
Methods **E**

STATISTICAL DOCUMENT

Cataloguing data can be found at the end of this publication

Luxembourg: Office for Official Publications of the European Communities, 1996

ISBN 92-827-7240-3

© ECSC-EEC-EAEC, Brussels • Luxembourg, 1996
Reproduction is authorized, except for commercial purposes, provided the source is acknowledged

Printed in Germany

Printed on non-chlorine bleached paper

Preface

It is now over thirty-five years since the first attempt was made in 1960 to collect comparable data on employment and unemployment from all six Member States of the then European Community by means of a labour force survey. Since that date, the number of Member States has risen to fifteen and the character of the European labour market has been transformed by the radical changes which have taken place, for example in activity rates, in the allocation of working-time, and in the distribution of employment across the various sectors of the economy.

Throughout this period, the institutions of the European Union have included the issues of employment and unemployment among their highest priorities. Both the economic and the social implications of recent trends in these areas have been regularly examined at meetings of the Council of Europe, which has repeatedly stressed the importance of monitoring such developments. The demand for accurate and comparable information on the labour market has consequently become progressively more urgent.

In this context, the rôle of the EU Labour Force Survey has gained steadily in importance, and is now universally recognised as an indispensable tool for observing labour market developments and for taking the appropriate policy measures. The LFS is the only source of information in these areas to provide data which is truly comparable in the sense of being independent of the national administrative and legislative framework. Among the statistical instruments available in the European Union, the LFS is unique for the sample-size it covers, for the length of the time-series which it offers, and for the unrivalled picture it can provide of economic and social developments from the very earliest days of the European Community right up to the present day.

During the lifetime of the survey, the need has also been recognised to be continually alert for any adaptations needed to meet changes in information requirements. The general methodology employed, together with a host of details concerning the definitions used and the practical implementation, have therefore been subject to continual evolution. Eurostat, which is responsible for the dissemination of the results of the survey at European Union level, has been conscious that accurate and up-to-date information on these aspects is indispensable to interpretation of the results. This information has therefore been published on a regular basis under the title *Labour Force Survey : Methods and Definitions*, of which several editions, documenting the successive changes made, have appeared in 1977, 1985, 1988 and 1992.

Labour Force Survey : Methods and Definitions, 1992 series marked the beginning of a new series of surveys which incorporated a number of important methodological changes. Since it was published, there have been no modifications to the content of the survey as such, but certain amendments have been introduced into the definitions and classification systems used, whilst the entry into the European Union of three new Member States from 1995 has involved some organisational changes. Such changes are recorded in this edition, and a new section has been added in order to expand the information provided on the operation of the surveys at national level.

Eurostat wishes to thank the experts responsible for the national labour force surveys in the Member States for their help in compiling this methodological information on the operation of the European Union Labour Force Survey. Their contributions were collected and edited by Esther Körmendi of Danmarks Statistik, whose secondment to Eurostat formed part of a long tradition of active involvement by the national statistical offices in the operation of the survey at EU level. The text was checked and revised by the late Dr Hildegard Fürst, as her last contribution to the project with which she had been closely associated from its inception thirty-five years previously. The final preparation of this publication was the responsibility of members of the Eurostat team covering labour market issues, Unit E-1, in particular Geoffrey Thomas and Neil Bain.

Contents

	Page
Labour force surveys in the European Union	
The purpose of labour force surveys	7
The history of labour force surveys	8
The development of the EU Labour Force Survey	8
The organisation of the EU Labour Force Survey	9
Data collection and diffusion of results	10
Technical features of the EU Labour Force Survey	
Field of the Survey	11
Reference period	11
Units of measurement	11
Reliability of the results	11
Comparability of results between countries	11
Comparability of results between successive surveys	12
Basic concepts and definitions	12
Characteristics of the national surveys	15
Tables	
1: Sample design	27
2: Data collection and data processing	28
3: Implementation of the household concept	30
EU list of questions	31
Annexes	
1: Regional codes used in the EU Labour Force Survey [based on the Nomenclature of Territorial Units (NUTS)]	47
2: Statistical Classification of Economic Activities (NACE Rev. 1)	53
3: International Standard Classification of Occupations [ISCO-88 (COM)]	55
4: Codification of countries	57
5: Attainment levels in education and training	59
Explanatory notes to the EU list of questions	63
Council Regulation (EEC) No 3711/91 of 16 December 1991 on the organisation of the EU Labour Force Survey	73
Bibliographical note	76

Labour force surveys in the European Union

The purpose of labour force surveys

A labour force survey is an inquiry directed to households designed to obtain information on the labour market and related issues by means of personal interviews. As it would clearly involve considerable expense to include all households (as in population censuses) labour force surveys are usually confined to a sample of households, the actual size of which depends primarily on the level of detail required in the survey estimates.

There are a number of advantages in using an approach of this kind in collecting labour market information. In the first place it affords the opportunity to obtain information on relevant labour market aspects across all sectors of the economy in a consistent manner. It also facilitates the interpretation of the information in a wider population setting, since the information collected need not necessarily be confined to persons in the labour force (i.e. those employed or unemployed), but can involve all other persons in the households covered. In current labour market circumstances this is an important additional dimension as analysis is increasingly concerned with those on the peripheries of the labour market.

In recent decades the borderline between the labour force and what is termed the «economically inactive» population has become increasingly blurred, due to the increasing incidence of part-time and temporary work and the ease with which large numbers of persons (particularly women and young persons in the final stages of their education) repeatedly enter or leave the labour force. Furthermore, the emergence of mass unemployment and long-term unemployment have resulted in a great many individuals becoming «marginalized» in the sense that they tend to lose tangible contact with the core labour market. The wider coverage associated with labour force surveys also allows the possibility of assessing labour market effects in a household or family context. This is important if, for example, one wishes to measure the extent to which persons other than those directly involved (e.g. spouses, other dependents, etc.) are affected by the circumstances of unemployment.

Another advantage of a labour force survey is that it affords the opportunity to define certain labour market characteristics not normally available from other statistical sources. Thus, for example, it is possible to identify the degree of employment engaged in by an individual in terms of the hours worked, or attempt to conceptualize unemployment in terms of aspects such as job search and availability for work. This is important because of the advantages it confers in being able to define certain labour market entities in a more meaningful way. Additionally, because the definitions used to measure these entities are the same for each country, comparability between Member States is guaranteed for certain estimates. This aspect is clearly of considerable importance in the context of the European Union.

There are however some limitations which apply to labour force surveys. Cost considerations place a constraint on the overall household sample size and the resultant sampling variability limits the level of detail that can reasonably be shown. Thus, for example, while the labour force survey can be used to compile estimates of employment across economic sectors, it cannot be expected to yield reliable figures at a detailed level of regional disaggregation, nor for individual small industrial or commercial subsectors. The sampling base on which such estimates would depend would be too small, and the degree of variability correspondingly high. For the same reason, there is also a limit to what can be achieved with labour force surveys in monitoring trends over time (in employment and unemployment, for example), especially if the movements involved are relatively small.

It is appropriate at this point to refer briefly to other sources of statistical information so that the position of the labour force survey in an overall statistical perspective can be more clearly understood. The other principal sources of labour market information are :
(a) surveys of enterprises
(b) administrative records.
The former source clearly has the potential for providing detailed estimates of employment for individual sectors (and in fact this is done in many countries). However, such a source is clearly restricted to a consideration of those with jobs and cannot provide any information on the unemployed, nor other persons outside the labour force but who may have an attachment to it. Such surveys can, however, be used to obtain information, not only in relation to employment, but also to output, earnings and hours worked. The simultaneous collection of consistent data on employment and output makes it possible to compile indicators of productivity. Indeed, the derivation of output-type information is usually the main purpose of enterprise-based surveys. Many countries, for example, carry out detailed quarterly or monthly inquiries of the industrial sector which provide consistent information on output, earnings, employment and other related aspects.

Administrative records, such as social insurance records or population registers as widely used in Denmark, Sweden and Finland, can also be used to provide indicators of the levels of employment and unemployment. A prerequisite, however, is that the administrative arrangements should specifically cater for the extraction of the relevant statistics. While this source involves relatively less expense than information derived from either enterprise or household surveys, it suffers from a significant disadvantage in that the underlying systems are based on social welfare or other administrative provisions which may not necessarily accord with the accepted conventions for defining employment and unemployment. Furthermore, if these arrangements are changed (and experience indicates that they frequently are), discontinuity invariably arises in the data. A disadvantage of even greater relevance in an international or EU context is the fact that the social insurance systems in question vary greatly from country to country, both in terms of their design and in the manner of their implementation. This renders the derived information virtually useless in the context of making comparisons between countries, especially in absolute terms. Such sources can, however, provide a reasonable basis for monitoring short-term (i.e. monthly, quarterly, etc.) trends, the most notable in this regard being the various national series on the registered unemployed.

To summarize, therefore, the principal advantages associated with labour force surveys relate to
(1) the opportunity of obtaining comprehensive information (at less cost than a census) across the entire economy, which can be assessed in a global setting embracing society as a whole;
(2) the inherent flexibility of such surveys, which makes it possible to define or conceptualize not only employment and unemployment, but also the circumstances surrounding other groups outside or on the margins of the labour force.
This latter feature (i.e. the facility to conceptualize or define) has assumed greater importance in recent years because of the manner in which labour markets and society have generally evolved, and in view of the growing need to view labour market phenomena in an international context. It must be recognized, however, that the sampling aspect associated with labour force surveys places a limitation on the level of detail possible when analysing the results.

The history of labour force surveys

The notion of obtaining information on the work force by means of household-based inquiries is not in any sense new. Questions on the concept of possessing a «gainful occupation» were introduced in censuses of population in some countries during the latter half of the last century. However, at that stage no questions were asked in regard to what is termed a person's «economic status», i.e. whether at work, unemployed or economically inactive. Indeed, at that stage such a notion was hardly even conceived. However, the advancing trend of industrialization and the resultant restructuring of society created a need for new approaches, and for more sophistication in measuring labour market phenomena. The situation became particularly urgent with the advent of mass unemployment in the 1930's following the Great Depression. Whatever the uncertainties that may have previously existed regarding the need to conceptualize or measure unemployment were dispelled by the sheer fact of millions in a state of enforced idleness. There was now a clear need to have regular information on the level and trend of employment and unemployment. The first labour force survey was introduced in the United States in 1940 (on a monthly basis) with a new conceptual framework designed to provide information on relevant labour market characteristics.

The movement towards the use of labour force surveys was somewhat slower in Europe. While the intervention of the war years contributed to this, it was also due to the existence of alternative sources of information which provided at least a partial insight into aspects of the labour force. Virtually all Western European countries maintained comprehensive unemployment registers (for the purpose of dispensing unemployment compensation) which, despite their disadvantages, provided a rudimentary basis for monitoring unemployment trends. However, in time, as the need to take a more global view of the labour market became apparent, different European countries began to initiate labour force surveys. The first European country to carry out a labour force survey was France in 1950. Further such inquiries were conducted in France throughout the subsequent decade and these evolved into a regular consistent series in the early 1960s. After an extended period of preparation, the Federal Republic of Germany initiated an annual series of labour force surveys in 1957 (the *Mikrozensus*). Sweden conducted its first labour force survey in 1959 and, after further experimentation, initiated a quarterly series in 1963.

The development of the EU Labour Force Survey

The first attempt to carry out a labour force survey covering the then European Community was made in 1960 with the six original Member States (Belgium, Germany, France, Italy, Luxembourg and the Netherlands). This was regarded largely as an experiment and was not repeated until 1968, when the first of a series of annual surveys took place. This ran for four years but in none of these were all six Member States covered, since Luxembourg defaulted in 1968 and the Netherlands from 1969 to 1971. With the enlargement of the European Community in 1973, a series of biennial surveys was initiated. The United Kingdom was the only one of the three new Member States to join the original six in the 1973 survey, but Ireland and Denmark also took part in 1975, 1977, 1979 and 1981. In this last year Greece took part as a new Member State for the first time but Luxembourg was not covered.

The definitions used in these early surveys were necessarily somewhat imprecise, due to the lack of an internationally accepted terminology. This gap was filled in 1982 when the Thirteenth International Conference of Labour Statisticians, convened at Geneva by the International Labour Organisation, passed a *Resolution concerning statistics of the economically active population, employment, unemployment and underemployment*, containing exact definitions of the various categories of the population which labour force surveys were designed to measure. The Member States of the then European Community agreed to apply these recommendations in a new series of Community Labour Force Surveys which would be conducted annually.

During the course of this series, from 1983 to 1991, a substantial and coherent database of labour market information was built up. This comprised microdata (individual observations) from ten Member States from 1983 onwards (with the exception of the Netherlands in 1984 and 1986), and from the new members Spain and Portugal from 1987. The number of households covered averaged between 500,000 and 600,000. The list of variables included remained virtually unchanged during this period (two items on educational attainment being added from 1988 onwards). The 'ILO recommendations' contained in the 1982 Resolution together with the clarifications made at the Fourteenth International Conference of Labour Statisticians in 1987 gained increasing acceptance. The demand for international comparisons gradually raised the profile of these definitions even in Member States where other concepts continued to be used for national purposes.

The current series of surveys was introduced in 1992. The survey continued to be conducted annually, but for the first time a criterion of statistical reliability at regional level was introduced. The list of variables covered was revised, so as to include topics relevant to the Single Market (such as labour mobility across national boundaries), innovative working patterns (working at home, second jobs or other economic activity outside the traditional forty-hour week) and recent developments in the area of education and vocational training. The questions relating to job-search were revised so as to underpin the commitment to the ILO recommendations, particularly by implementing the distinction between active and non-active methods of seeking work. The continued commitment to the ILO recommendations ensured a high degree of comparability between the results obtained from this series and those from the surveys between 1983 and 1991.

Since 1995 the survey has covered fifteen Member States. Austria, Sweden and Finland all possessed well-established labour force surveys before their entry into the European Union (embedded in the national Mikrozensus in the case of Austria), but in each of these three cases some adjustments were necessary in order to maintain the level of comparability which had already been achieved between the other Member States.

In the mid-1990's a number of concurrent developments has become apparent. Technological advance has led to the increasing use of computers at all stages of data collection, and the introduction in several Member States of portable computers at the interview stage - Computer Assisted Personal Interviewing (CAPI) - is facilitating the emergence of a range of new techniques. In some Member States it is also possible and permissible to access other computer files such as registers, to supplement the information collected in the interviews. These developments facilitate the requirement for swifter and more up-to-date information, which in turn has created a tendency towards more frequent surveys. The descriptions of the national surveys presented later in this volume indicate that, in more than half the Member States, interviews are now conducted on a quarterly or monthly basis, and almost all those still conducting annual interviews are also at various stages of planning or implementing more frequent surveys. This tendency will be reflected in future European Union surveys, the format of which is now under discussion. The process of defining a target-structure for the EU Labour Force Survey, which will permit future developments in the Member States to proceed in a consistent and co-ordinated manner, has been under way since 1994 and will be completed in 1996.

The organisation of the EU Labour Force Survey

The earliest Community Labour Force Surveys were not covered by legislation, but, from 1973 onwards, a Regulation was passed by the Council of Ministers governing the operation of the survey. Each Regulation applied only to a single year's survey, until the surveys of 1990 and 1991 were included in one Regulation (Council Regulation (EEC) No. 3044/89). With the introduction of the new series from 1992 onwards, it was agreed to introduce a single Regulation (Council Regulation (EEC) No. 3711/91) to remain in force until explicitly replaced by new legislation. A copy of this latest Regulation is to be found towards the end of this publication.

The above Regulations stipulate the agreements reached by the Member States and Eurostat on the implementation of the survey. The technical aspects of the survey are discussed by Eurostat and representatives of the respective national statistical offices and employment ministries, meeting regularly (between one and three times a year) at the Employment Statistics Working Party held in Luxembourg. This Working Party determines the content of the survey, the EU list of questions and the common coding of individual replies, as well as the principal definitions to be applied for the analyses of the results.

The national statistical institutes are responsible for selecting the sample, preparing the questionnaires, conducting the direct interviews among households, and forwarding the results to Eurostat in accordance with the common coding scheme. Eurostat devises the programme for analysing the results and is responsible for processing and disseminating the information sent by the national statistical institutes.

The questionnaires are drawn up by each Member State in the national language or languages, taking into account the stipulations made in the Regulation. For every survey characteristic listed in the Regulation, a question or series of questions exists in each questionnaire to permit this information to be supplied to Eurostat. Otherwise the information is imputed from other sources such as population registers. The questionnaires may also contain other questions which do not relate to the list of characteristics in the Regulation, but rather reflect an interest in the topic concerned at national level. Based on the sample design the figures obtained from the sample survey are expanded to population levels, usually on the basis of grossing-up factors derived from the most recent census of population, suitably adjusted to take account of recent changes which may have occurred since that census.

The design of the sample is subject to certain constraints imposed in the Regulation concerning both the required level of statistical reliability and representativity at Regional level NUTS II. The Regulation also stipulates that a minimumum 4-wave rotation pattern be used (see Table 1). Within these constraints each Member State draws up its own sample design and carries out the interviews. In countries with a federal structure, such as Germany, regional statistical offices may exercise a considerable amount of autonomy in the data collection. The interviews have invariably been carried out in Spring, but the exact periods may vary considerably. The week-number of the reference week in which each household is interviewed is among the information collected, thus permitting seasonal adjustment to be carried out.

Data collection and diffusion of results

As soon as each Member State has completed its data collection and verification, the part pertaining to the EU Labour Force Survey is, if necessary, transcoded to Eurostat requirements and transmitted by magnetic support. Eurostat then checks the data for errors according to its own programme of controls. When the data are considered to be error-free they are converted into a SAS database, which can be easily accessed to produce reports. For reasons of confidentiality this database may only be accessed by accredited Eurostat personnel.

Most Member States produce regular publications setting out the results of their national surveys, details of which may be found in the bibliography at the end of this publication. The yearly report at EU level, which, as mentioned, is the responsibility of Eurostat, contains five main sections covering Population and activity, Employment, Working time, Unemployment and search for work, and Households. Some specific organisational and methodological notes are included in this publication, but, in the interests of rapid diffusion of the results, no attempt is made to analyse the data. From 1994 onwards a selection of graphs has been included in order to improve the presentation of the results. The 1995 results publication will include for the first time figures for the three new Member States - Austria, Finland and Sweden.

Detailed studies of labour market developments in the European Union may be found in the annual Commission report *Employment in Europe* and, in the wider context of the highly-developed countries, in the OECD's *Employment Outlook*. Data are supplied from the EU LFS database for these publications as well as for a plethora of other studies and reports at national and international level.

Within Eurostat, the richness of the EU Labour Force Survey, including its household dimension, causes it to be frequently used for general publications such as *Europe in Figures* and the *Social Portrait of Europe*. The EU LFS database is also occasionally used to provide data for the publication of Rapid Reports by other services of Eurostat. Among more specialised applications is the use of the database to produce comparable annual estimates of unemployment which, when combined with monthly national administrative data, provide comparable unemployment rates, as published in Eurostat's monthly bulletin *Unemployment in the European Union*. Additionally, the preparation of policy actions in the field of EU social and regional policy through the operation of the Structural Funds relies upon the availability of a solid base of comparable data from the EU Labour Force Survey.

The survey results are completely integrated into the Eurostat statistical system, so that they may be consulted for example through the New Cronos and Regio databases. Users with specific data requirements which are not satisfied by the existing publications and databases may also ask for specified tables to be produced on a chargeable basis. Several hundred such requests are received each year from different public and private bodies, research institutes, universities, etc. They may be addressed to the central Eurostat Information Office (+352-4301-34567; fax 4301-436404), and Eurostat is currently extending its data dissemination facilities, setting up Data Shops in every Member State.

The growing volume of this demand for information is an eloquent testimony to the central rôle of the Labour Force Survey in the European statistical system. In the field of social statistics there is no other instrument which provides information on social and economic developments within the European Union over such a long timespan, with such a large sample-size or with such a level of comparability.

Technical features of the EU Labour Force Survey

Field of the Survey

The survey is intended to cover the whole of the resident population, i.e. all persons whose usual place of residence is in the territory of the Member States of the European Union. For technical and methodological reasons, however, it is not possible in all countries to include the population living in collective households, i.e. persons living in homes, boarding schools, hospitals, religious institutions, workers' hostels, etc.

Consequently, for the purpose of harmonizing the field of survey, results are compiled for the population of private households only. This comprises all persons living in the households surveyed during the reference week, and those persons absent from the household for short periods due to studies, holidays, illness, business trips, etc.

It does not cover persons who, although having links with the household under survey:
(a) usually live in another household;
(b) live in collective households (in particular, persons doing compulsory military service are excluded from the population of private households and regarded as members of collective households, even if during the reference week they are present in the private household to which they belong);
(c) have emigrated.

Reference period

The labour force characteristics of each person interviewed refer to their situation in a particular week. While this reference week falls in Spring in all countries, the national statistical institutes determine the exact week(s) according to the particular situation in each country. The reference weeks used in the different Member States are shown in the yearly reports containing the survey results. As a general rule the reference week should be a normal week, i.e. it should exclude bank holidays. For countries using a fixed reference week, this requirement is easy to fulfil. In some countries, however, the survey extends over a period of time and, as the reference week is the one preceding the week of the interview, the reference week varies. In this case, the reference week may sometimes include public holidays, such as Easter.

Units of measurement

The main units of measurement for which results are obtained from the survey are individuals and households. The definition of a household varies somewhat from country to country but these differences are unlikely in the majority of cases to have a significant effect on the comparability of the results. More information on household coverage by Member State is given in table 3.

Reliability of the results

As with any sample survey, the results of the Labour Force Survey are subject to sampling errors. In addition, the results of any sample survey are affected by non-sampling errors, i.e. the whole variety of errors other then those due to sampling. These can be due to many factors such as inability or unwillingness of respondents to provide correct answers or even any answer at all (non-response), mistakes by interviewers when filling in survey documents, miscoding, etc. Methods exist to assess the influence of these non-sampling errors on the accuracy of the survey results, but being often costly, are not generally applied.

Experience shows that at national level the survey information provides sufficiently accurate estimates for the levels and structures of the various aggregates into which the labour force is divided, provided that analyses of this type are confined to levels of a certain size. Survey results at regional level may, however, be affected by considerable sampling errors, even for relatively large groups of the population. Reliability of the results is assured by the size of the samples and the sampling methods used, in addititon to careful and thorough planning of the various survey operations and rigorous administration of all phases of the survey.

Comparability of results between countries

Perfect comparability among 15 countries is difficult to achieve, even were it to be by means of a single direct survey, i.e. a survey carried out at the same time, using the same questionnaire and a single method of recording.

Nevertheless, the degree of comparability of the EU Labour Force Survey results is considerably higher than that of any other existing set of statistics on employment or unemployment available for Member States. This is due to:

(i) the recording of the same set of characteristics in each country;

(ii) a close correspondence between the EU list of questions and the national questionnaires;

(iii) the use of the same definitions for all countries;

(iv) the use of common classifications (e.g. NACE for economic activity);

(v) the synchronization of the survey in Spring;

(vi) the data being centrally processed by Eurostat.

The EU Labour Force Survey, although subject to the constraints of the EU's statistical requirements, is a joint effort by Member States to coordinate their national employment surveys, which must serve their own national requirements. Therefore, in spite of the close coordination between the national statistical institutes and Eurostat, there inevitably remain some differences in the survey from country to country.

Comparability of results between successive surveys

Since 1983 improved comparability between results of successive surveys has been achieved, mainly due to the greater stability of content and the higher frequency of surveys. However, the following factors may somewhat detract from perfect comparability:

(i) the population figures used for the population adjustment are revised at intervals on the basis of new population censuses;

(ii) the reference period may not remain the same for a given country;

(iii) in order to improve the quality of results, some countries may change the content or order of their questionnaire;

(iv) countries may modify their sample designs;

(v) the manner in which certain questions are answered may be influenced by the political or social circumstances at the time of interview.

As far as they are known, Eurostat indicates the main factors affecting the comparability of the data for successive surveys in the publications containing the results.

Basic concepts and definitions

The main statistical objectives of the Labour Force Survey is to divide the population of working age (15 years and above) into three mutually exclusive and exhaustive groups - persons in employment, unemployed persons and inactive persons - and to provide descriptive and explanatory data on each of these categories. Respondents are assigned to one of these groups on the basis of the most objective information possible obtained through the survey questionnaire, which principally relates to their actual activity within a particular reference week.

The section 'EU list of questions' together with the explanatory notes show how the survey questioning is organized. Most questions apply to selected groups only. A filter based on information already obtained normally specifies who should answer a particular question.

The definitions of employment and unemployment used in the Community Labour Force Survey closely follow those adopted by the 13th International Conference of Labour Statisticians.

The relevant parts of these 'ILO definitions' are:

'Employment

9.(1) The employed comprise all persons above a specified age who during a specified brief period, either one week or one day, were in the following categories:

(a) "paid employment":

(a1) "at work": persons who during the reference period performed some work for wage or salary, in cash or in kind;

(a2) "with a job but not at work": persons who, having already worked in their present job, were temporarily not at work during the reference period and had a formal attachment to their job. This formal job attachment should be determined in the light of national circumstances, according to one or more of the following criteria:

(i) the continued receipt of wage or salary;

(ii) an assurance of return to work following the end of the contingency, or an agreement as to the date of return;

(iii) the elapsed duration of absence from the job which, wherever relevant, may be that duration for which workers can receive compensation benefits without obligations to accept other jobs.

(b)"self-employment":

(b1)"at work": persons who during the reference period performed some work for profit or family gain, in cash or in kind;

(b2)"with an enterprise but not at work": persons with an enterprise, which may be a business enterprise, a farm or a service undertaking, who were temporarily not at work during the reference period for any specific reason.

9.(2)For operational purposes, the notion of "some work" may be interpreted as work for at least one hour.

Unemployment

10.(1)The "unemployed" comprise all persons above a specified age who, during the reference period, were:

(a)"without work", i.e. were not in paid employment or self-employment, as defined in paragraph 9;

(b)"currently available for work", i.e. were available for paid employment or self-employment during the reference period;

(c)"seeking work", i.e. had taken specific steps in a specified recent period to seek paid employment or self-employment'.

In applying these definitions to the EU Labour Force survey, the following reference periods are implemented:

(i)In paragraph 10(b) "currently available" should mean available to start work within two weeks of the reference period.

(ii)In paragraph 10(c) the "specified recent period" is the four weeks preceding the survey interview. During this period at least one active method to find work should be undertaken in order to satisfy the criterion of "seeking work".

Unemployed persons can be classified by reason for unemployment into four major groups:

(1)job-losers are persons whose employment ended involuntarily and immediately began looking for work;
(2)job-leavers are persons who quit or otherwise terminated their employment voluntarily and immediately began looking for work;
(3)re-entrants are persons who previously worked, but were inactive or on compulsory military service before beginning to look for work;
(4)first job-seekers are persons who have never worked in a regular job.

Labour force
The labour force comprises persons in employment and unemployed persons.

Inactive persons
All persons who are not classified as employed or unemployed are defined as inactive. Apart from showing pupils and students separately, no further breakdown is provided for this group. Conscripts on compulsory military or community service are excluded from the compilation of the survey results.

The above groups are used to derive the following measures:

(a)*Activity rates*
Activity rates represent the labour force as a percentage of the population of working age (15 years or more).

(b)*Employment / population ratios*
Employment / population ratios represent persons in employment as a percentage of the population of working age (15 years or more).

(c)*Unemployment rates*
Unemployment rates represent unemployed persons as a percentage of the labour force.

(d)*Duration of unemployment*
defined as the shorter of the following two periods
(a)the duration of search for work, or
(b)the length of time since last employment.

The above rates are usually calculated for sex-age groups and are sometimes further cross-classified by other demographic variables such as marital status or nationality.

Labour force classification in the European Union Labour Force Survey

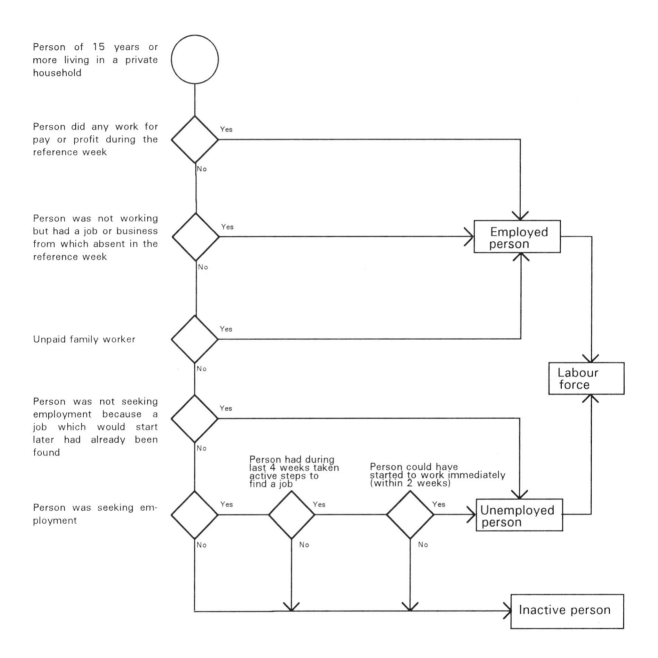

Characteristics of the national surveys

BELGIQUE / BELGIE

Background

The Belgian Labour Force Survey is intended to provide information on the structure of the active population and short term trends in the labour market. National obligations to fulfill the EU Regulation are laid down by law. Participation in the whole survey is compulsory.
The survey is carried out yearly during the spring and serves both national and EU purposes. It provides annual results at both national and regional level. The survey is planned to be conducted quarterly from 1997.
The survey is carried out in all regions.
Both private and collective households are surveyed.
The same reference week is used for all interviews.

Sample design

The sampling frame consists of population registers, restricted to heads of household.
The sample is stratified by province (with Brabant province divided into north and south). The sampling ratio varies between provinces. For the larger provinces the target sample size is proportional to the square root of the population. This gives a balance between accuracy at the provincial and national level. The sample in Brussels is increased by 2,000 households. Smaller provinces are over-sampled to give a minimum sample size of 2,000 households in order to provide reliable estimates.
The primary sample units are based on pre-1977 communes. Within each province, PSU's are selected with a probability proportional to the number of households they contain. In total 700 PSU's are selected.
The secondary sample units are households.
Within each PSU, 50 households are sampled systematically. Thus 35,000 households are selected in all. Each year 30% of the PSU's selected in the previous year are randomly selected and the 50 households interviewed the previous year are re-interviewed.

Weighting procedure

A single stage post-stratification by age-band, sex and "arrondissement administratif" with control totals based is applied on independent estimates of the population at the start of the year. As the arrondissements combine to form the provinces the weighting procedure implicitly corrects for the different sampling ratios between provinces.

Questionnaire

The questionnaire consists of two parts:
    household questionnaire
    individual questionnaire.
The household questionnaire contains identification of the reference person and data on the household size and type of household.
The individual questionnaire contains exclusively questions included in the EU LFS.
Additional codes are included in the following EU questions:
    type of professional status
    part time work
    working hours
    reasons for leaving last job or business.
Complementary data from the population register include
    country of residence
    region one year before the survey
    degree of urbanization.
The questionnaire does not contain questions but is in keyword format.

DANMARK

Background

The Danish Labour Force Survey was conducted with varying frequency and methods from 1967. In the fourth quarter of 1993 the Unemployment Survey was integrated into the Danish LFS, and both surveys have since been conducted quarterly.
There is no specific national legislation concerning obligation to provide information for the survey, and participation in the survey is voluntary.
Up to 1993 annual results were published at national and regional level. From 1994 onwards quarterly results are published at national level and annual results at regional level.
The whole country is covered, excluding Greenland and the Faeroe Islands.
Both private and collective households are surveyed.
Data for the purpose of the EU LFS is collected in the second quarter of the year. Up to 1993 the reference weeks were spread over a five month period. From 1994 onwards the reference weeks are evenly spread throughout the year.

Sample design

The sample is based upon a household (D-Family) living at the same address. A D-family may consist of a single person or a couple, along with any children. A maximum of two generations in a family may be represented in a D-family. If three generations live in the same dwelling the grandparents form a separate family unit.

The sampling frame consists of the Current Population Register (CPR).

No stratification was used up to 1993. From 1994 the registered unemployed are over-sampled.

Up to 1993 a single stage sample was selected at the beginning of the year consisting of just over 14,000 D-families. From 1994 quarterly samples of 15,600 persons are drawn from the Current Population Register (CPR).

Up to 1993 a three wave rotation pattern was used. Persons were interviewed three times at annual intervals, with one third of the sample being replaced each year. From 1994 the selected individuals have been interviewed 3 times in subsequent quarters, and once more one year after the last interview.

Weighting procedure

Up to 1993 a post-stratification was carried out by sex, age, region, family type and whether registered unemployed. The sample estimates were based upon the aggregates taken from the CPR at the same time as the sample was drawn.

From 1994 post stratification is carried out by age band, sex, sector of activity, vocational education, registered unemployment and income.

Questionnaire

Up to 1993 the content of the Danish Labour Force Survey was almost identical with the 1992 EU codification. Data was collected by interview, apart from information on demographic background which was derived from the Central Population Register.

Since the integration of the Danish LFS with the Unemployment survey in 1994, the questionnaire contains a great number of additional questions. The questionnaire is identical in all quarters and for all waves. Data are only collected by questionnaires from the selected individuals in the sample. For other household members information is derived from the CPR as concerns demographic background and educational attainment level, and imputed as regards the remaining information.

There is no household questionnaire.

Additional information for national purposes at individual level includes the following:

In the LFS part of the survey:
all causes for differences between usual and normal working hours are registered separately with specification of the number of hours due to the specific cause. Question on usual hours in second job.

In the unemployment part of the survey:
exhaustive information on unemployment periods, type of unemployment (partial, full-time), type of benefit, actions taken by authorities, etc.

All information concerning demographic background including nationality, degree of urbanisation, type of household and educational level is derived from administrative registers.

As data is collected by CATI, a great number of questions have alternative wording depending on the responses to preceding questions.

DEUTSCHLAND

Background

The German LFS is conducted within the framework of the annual Mikrozensus which was set up in 1957. The main objective of the survey is to provide information on the living conditions of the population, and to furnish data on employment and unemployment which is comparable with other countries in the Community.

Legislation of January 1996 "Gesetz zur Durchführung einer Repräsentativstatistik über die Bevölkerung und den Arbeitsmarkt sowie die Wohnsituation der Haushalte (Mikrozensusgesetz)" lays down the principle of obligation to provide information for the purpose of production of the Mikrozensus. The Mikrozensus consists of a compulsory as well as a voluntary part.

The survey produces annual results at national and regional level.

Both private and collective households are sampled. There is a single reference week.

Sample design

Sample districts consist of a number of dwellings.

All persons within a selected sample district are interviewed. There are five types of sample districts:

(a) a number of buildings near to each other (but not necessarily adjacent), each containing less than five dwellings. The target size for this group is 12 dwellings.

(b) a single building containing 5 to 10 dwellings.

(c) a sub-division of a building containing 11 or more dwellings. Buildings containing 11 or more dwellings are sub-divided with a target size of 6 dwellings.

(d) newly constructed dwellings. New sample districts are formed from a group of buildings, a single building or a subdivision of a building with a target size of 6 dwellings.

(e) a group of people living in a collective household. The target size for this group is 15 people.

The sample districts in the first group are, on average, larger than in the other groups in order to reduce interviewers' travelling time and hence reduce costs.

For the old Länder the sampling frame is based on the 1987 census records, updated with new dwellings.

For the new Länder, the data in the central population registers are reduced according to the number of persons and number of households at each address. The frame is updated annually using statistical returns on new building.

The stratification by region and size of buildings is based on the size classes used to construct the sampling units. The sampling fraction varies between regions. Within each stratum a stratification-like effect results by systematically sampling from a list sorted by geographical location.

Regions are formed with on average 350,000 inhabitants. The list of sample districts is sorted within each stratum by subregion, Kreis (administrative district), commune size class, commune and sample district number. This list is divided into groups of 100 consecutive sample districts. One sample is chosen at random from each of these groups to give a 1% sample for the Microzensus. A systematic sub sample of this 1% sample is used for the LFS. To achieve the required sampling error at NUTS II level (as set out in the regulation) the sub-sampling fraction varies, being either 100%, 80%, 60% or 40%, giving overall sampling fractions of 1%, 0.8%, 0.6% or 0.4%. Overall the sampling fraction averages around 0.45%.

A four wave rotation pattern is used. Each sample unit remains in the sample for four years, with 25% of the sample being replaced each year.

Weighting procedure

A two stage adjustment process is used:
(i) Where possible, limited data is collected for households that do not respond. This data can include: size of household; whether of German nationality; and, for one person households, age (whether under 60 or 60 and over) and sex. Using this data, the weights of responding households are increased to take account of non-response within regions.
(ii) The sample, weighted for non-response, is post-stratified by region, sex and nationality (German/non-German), and grossed up to the population data (adjusted for military personnel).

Questionnaire

The questionnaire consists of compulsory and voluntary questions. The majority of the items collected for the EU LFS are compulsory.

The household questionnaire contains number of persons in the household, changes in the size and composition of the household since the previous survey, age of the dwelling.

A number of additional questions for national purposes are included in the questionnaire:
    Attendance at kindergarten, school, vocational school, technical university, university
    Pension and nursing care insurance
    Income and sources of livelihood.

ELLADA

Background

The first series of surveys concerning the Greek labour market situation of the population was conducted in the period 1974-1980. From 1981 the LFS was integrated into the EU LFS.

A common decision is issued every year by the Minister of Finance and the Minister of Economy concerning the approval and conduct of the LFS. Participation in the survey is compulsory.

The survey is carried out annually in the second quarter and serves both national and Community purposes. From 1997 it is planned to carry out the survey quarterly. The survey produces annual results at national and regional level.

The survey covers only private households.

The reference weeks are spread over a period of 15 weeks.

Sample design

The sampling units are as follows:
(i) Primary sampling unit are localities.
(ii) Secondary sample units are city blocks, or, in rural areas, census enumeration districts.
(iii) Tertiary sample units are dwellings.
All households within a selected dwelling are surveyed.

The sampling frame for the primary and secondary sampling is based on the previous census and shows the number of households in each city block or enumeration district. Below this level interviewers compile lists of households in the selected areas.

Stratification is carried out by administrative region by degree of urbanization. The localities of the country (apart from Greater Salonica and Greater Athens) are put into one of 8 strata depending on the size of population of the locality. These strata are further divided by the nine administrative regions. Greater Salonica and Greater Athens are divided into, 10 and 40 respectively, equally sized strata.

For the strata composed of localities with fewer than 10,000 inhabitants, a sample of localities is selected with probability proportional to size. In the other strata all localities are sampled.

Within each selected locality, including all localities with a population of 10,000 or more, a predetermined number of areas (either city blocks or enumeration areas) is selected, with probability proportional to size.

The interviewer makes a list of all the occupied dwellings in the selected enumeration areas or city blocks, then selects a systematic sample from this list with the sampling interval calculated in such a way as to yield the specified sampling fraction for each strata. In all 61,000 households are selected.

A four wave rotation pattern is used. Each sample unit remains in the sample for four years with 25% of the sample being replaced each year.

Weighting procedure

Households which do not respond are substituted by the next household on the enumeration list.
No post stratification is carried out. The weighting factor related to population adjustment is such that, at national level, the survey population estimates are identical to the official independent population estimates.

Questionnaire

In addition to the information collected for the EU LFS the questionnaire also contains questions on external migration for the 5 previous years. The questionnaire is divided into two parts:
> household questionnaire
> individual questionnaire

The household questionnaire contains demographic background and educational attainment level for all household members.
The individual questionnaire contains not only the information specified in the EU codification but also the following additional data for national purposes:
> number of days worked in reference week in main job
> number of days worked in reference week in second job
> unsociable hours in second job
> work at home in second job
> household members residing abroad.

ESPAÑA

Background

The Spanish LFS is a quarterly survey which has been conducted by the INS since 1964. The main aim of the survey is to give estimates of the main labour market aggregates and to follow the evolution of the labour market.
The legislation relating to surveys in Spain does not make it obligatory to provide information for the survey. Participation in the survey is voluntary.
Data for the EU LFS is collected in the second quarter of each year.
The survey produces quarterly results at national and regional level (NUTS II and NUTS III).
The survey covers Mainland Spain, the Balearics, the Canary Islands, Ceuta and Melilla.
Only private households are covered.
The reference weeks are evenly distributed throughout the year with the exception of August.

Sample design

The sampling units are as follows:-
(i) Primary Sampling Units which are sub-divisions of municipal districts (statistical sections). Each section has a population of between 500 and 2,000 registered voters.
(ii) Secondary Sampling Units which are private dwellings.
The first stage sampling frame is a list of the PSU's. The second stage sampling frame is a list of the postal addresses of all the dwellings in the selected sections. The list of the sections is updated with census information. The list of dwellings in the selected sections is updated every six quarters by the interviewers.
Stratification is carried out in each province by degree of urbanization of the municipality. These are further divided into sub-strata using information on the predominant socio-economic status of the population of the section taken from the preceding census or municipal register.
(i) The number of sections selected from each province is a compromise between uniform and proportional allocation, so as to achieve a balance between the accuracy of data at provincial and national level. Within each province the allocation of sections within strata is proportional to population except for larger municipalities which are slightly over-represented. Within each sub-stratum the required number of sections are selected with probability proportional to the number of households according to the last census. 3,216 sections are selected in all.
(ii) In each section an average of 20 dwellings are selected by drawing a systematic sample with random start-point from the list of dwellings in the section. Thus, approximately 64,000 dwellings are selected in all.
A six wave rotation pattern is used with dwellings remaining in the sample for six successive quarters. The selected statistical selections are not rotated, but a new selection of PSU's is made with the information from the Census. Every quarter, in one sixth of the sampled sections, the existing sample of households is discarded and a new sample is drawn.

Weighting procedure

For each stratum, estimates are made of the population aged 0-15 and 16 and over. Within the strata uniform weights are applied to all the adults in the survey so that the total of the weights is equal to the population estimates, and similarly for children.

Questionnaire

Data are collected throughout the year (except August) with identical questionnaires. Questions concerning the situation one year ago with regard to activity, country and region of residence are only asked in the second quarter.
The questionnaire is divided into four parts:
> Identification questionnaire
> Household questionnaire
> Individual questionnaire for persons under 16 years
> Individual questionnaire for persons aged 16 years and over.

The identification questionnaire contains:
- Identification of the dwelling
- Identification of the interviewer
- Information concerning the previous interview.

The household questionnaire contains a list of the members of the household, relation to reference person, presence/absence of the individual during the reference week, duration of presence/absence, if the person is living in another family dwelling, age, number of persons within the dwelling.

The individual questionnaire contains for persons under the age of 16 years:
- demographic background information
- two questions concerning paid work.

In second quarter only:
- migration in relation to one year ago.

For persons aged 16 years and over:
- Some additional questions or extended response categories for national purposes in questions included in EU LFS.

Additional information for national purposes includes:
- position or function in the job
- name of the enterprise
- type of temporary work contract
- working hours (break for lunch or not)
- acceptance of job under specific conditions (change of residence, profession, etc.)
- field of public sector.

Information concerning personal data, occupation and economic activity is carried over from previous interviews.

From 1996 the interviews will be carried out by hand held computers.

FRANCE

Background

The French LFS has been conducted since 1950 with varying methods and frequency. Traditionally the design, the methods and the questionnaire have been modified in connection with Censuses of Population.
Participation in the survey is compulsory.
The survey is carried out annually in the Spring and serves both national and Community purposes.
The survey covers only metropolitan France.
Only private households are included.
The reference weeks are concentrated in a four week period.

Sample design

The sample is drawn in four stages:
(i) Primary sample units are rural cantons or urban units.
(ii) Secondary sample units in rural areas, and in urban areas with fewer than 10,000 inhabitants, are communes. Communes containing less than 160 dwellings are combined with neighbouring communes. Census districts are the basis of the SSU's in urban areas. However, due to the large variation in the size of census districts, smaller census districts are merged with similar neighbouring districts to produce units with approximately 1,000 dwellings, or 500 dwellings if the urban unit has a population greater than 100,000.
(iii) The tertiary sampling units consist of an area containing a number of dwellings. To improve the efficiency of the sample by reducing the degree of clustering, the TSU's in large urban areas contain fewer dwellings than the TSU's in other areas. In rural areas and in urban areas with a population of less than 100,000, the tertiary sampling units consist of areas containing approximately 160 dwellings. In urban areas with a population greater than 100,000, the tertiary sampling units contain approximately 80 dwellings. To make the TSU's as heterogeneous as possible, and thus reduce the loss in efficiency due to the use of an area sample, the TSU's are selected so that they are all as alike as possible in terms of housing.
(iv) The TSU's are divided into four equally sized areas to enable sample rotation. Buildings constructed since the census are included in the area sample if there are less than 10 new dwellings. If there are ten or more new dwellings, the new buildings are grouped into sample units of approximately ten dwellings.

Census documents and maps are used to identify all the buildings in the secondary sampling units and to divide the SSU's into tertiary sampling units.

Building permits are used as the source of information on new constructions.

The PSU's are divided into 210 strata, formed by crossing the 21 regions by 10 levels of urbanization. New constructions of 10 dwellings or more form a separate stratum in each region.

The sample structure is as follows:
(i) The number of areas sampled in each strata is determined by dividing the number of dwellings in the strata (according to the last census) by the product of the sampling ratio (300) and the number of dwellings per area (20 in large urban areas, otherwise 40). A systematic sample is drawn from a list of all the dwellings taken from the census to select the PSU's and for the larger PSU's to give the number of areas to be selected.
(ii) The SSU's in each PSU are then grouped so that there are the same number of groups as SSU's to be selected. From each of these groups one SSU is selected with probability proportional to population.
(iii) The third stage of sampling is to select the areas to be sampled, with the probability of selection proportional to the number of dwellings in each area. A total of 1,845 areas of 80 dwellings are selected in large urban areas, and 1,425 areas of 160 dwellings in rural and smaller urban areas.
(iv) One of the four subdivisions of a selected TSU is then sampled with each subdivision having equal likelihood of being chosen. In 1993 a total of 78,385 dwellings were selected.

The annual survey has a three wave structure with each group of 20 or 40 dwellings staying in the sample for 3 years with one third of the sample being replaced each year. When a group of dwellings leaves the sample it is replaced by another group from the same TSU.

Weighting procedures

A two stage adjustment procedure is used.
(i) The first stage adjusts for non-response by post stratifying by degree of urbanization, by whether first, second or third interview, and weighting the responses in each strata by the reciprocal of the response rate for that strata.
(ii) The second stage uses a generalized "Raking Ratio" method to adjust the weight for each household so that the survey estimates agree with independent population estimates for sex by five year age band. This method ensures that individual and household analyses give consistent results.

Questionnaire

The questionnaire consists of :
    a household questionnaire
    an individual questionnaire.
The household questionnaire includes
    the type of accommodation,
    number of rooms, household composition
    demographic background of the
    individual / household members.
The individual questionnaire contains a number of questions for national purposes in addition to the information specified in the EU codification.
The following questions are for national purposes:
    main status
    changes in main status from month to
    month in the year previous to the interview
    how person found current employment
    underemployment
    income.
Complementary data is used from the previous survey.
Since 1995 all data have been collected by CAPI.

IRELAND

Background

The Irish LFS has been conducted annually since 1983. To ensure reasonable continuity with the former Census-based estimates before the advent of the LFS, the Irish CSO publishes two sets of estimates, one based on the individual respondent's own assessment of his/her Principal Economic Status and another based on the current concepts of ILO.
There is no specific legislation concerning obligation to provide information for the survey. Participation in the survey is voluntary.

The survey is conducted annually and serves both national and EU purposes. It is under consideration to change the design and carry out the survey quarterly. All regions are covered.
Both private and collective households are included.
The reference weeks are spread over 8 to 9 weeks, although concentrated in a 4 week period.

Sample design

The sample is drawn in two stages.
Primary sampling units are based on Enumeration Areas from the previous census. These contain approximately 300 households. In large towns (>5,000 populations) and mixed urban/rural areas bordering these towns, the enumeration areas are split into areas containing about 75 households. In other areas the Enumeration Areas form the PSU's.
Secondary sampling units are households.
A sampling frame for the PSU's is provided by the two previous censuses. Below this level the interviewers compile lists of households within selected PSU's which are used for the secondary sampling.
Strata are formed by crossing counties with the level of urbanization. This gives 171 strata in all. The sampling fraction varies between these strata.
The sample structure is as follows:
A sample of PSU's are selected from each of the 171 strata. Of the 8,200 PSU's in Ireland, 1,076 are selected.
The interviewer draws up a list of the households in the selected PSU's, and a systematic sample from this list. The sampling interval varies depending on the number of households currently in the interviewer's area. In all some 50,000 households are selected.
Whilst drawing up the list of households within a PSU, the interviewer also identifies non-private households and determines the usual number of residents. A sample of non-private households with 15 or fewer residents is selected and the residents interviewed. In all non-private households containing 15 or more residents, a sample of the residents is interviewed. 283 collective households were included in the 1993 sample.
In general, respondents are only interviewed once. However 25% of the sample is retained from one year to the next in order to meet EU requirements.

Weighting procedure

A three-stage adjustment and grossing process is used.
(i) Within each PSU each household has a factor attached which is the ratio of the number of households listed in the PSU to the number of households interviewed.
(ii) For each of the 171 strata, the weights are multiplied by a factor so that the weights for the strata sum to the total population recorded in the 1991 census.

(iii) As a final stage the sample is post-stratified by Planning Region, age band, sex and the results from stage two, constrained to independent population estimates for this post stratification.

Questionnaire

Besides labour market information for national and EU purposes, the Irish LFS collects a wide range of data concerning housing. One questionnaire per household contains housing, household and individual information.

The questionnaire contains relatively detailed information concerning housing and a few additional items for national purposes concerning the labour market situation of the individual.

Housing:
    type of accommodation
    number of rooms
    age and heating of dwelling
    rent paid.

Labour market:
    main status
    membership of trade union
    injury at work
    illness or disability at work
    number of days lost.

No complementary data from other sources are used. The questionnaire does not contain questions, being in keyword format.

ITALIA

Background

The Italian LFS is an independent survey, carried out quarterly since 1959, with the aim of furnishing actual information on the current situation and short term trends in the labour market.

The principle of obligation to provide information for the survey is supported by law. Participation is compulsory in the whole survey.

Data for the EU LFS are collected in April each year with a slightly extended version of the national questionnaire.

The survey produces quarterly results at national and regional level.

All provinces (103) are covered.

Only private households are included.

A single reference week is used each quarter.

Sample design

The sample is drawn in two stages:
(i) Primary sample units are the municipalities.
(ii) Secondary sampling units are registered households.

The sampling frame consists of the municipal registers.

Stratification of municipalities within provinces is by population of the strata (municipality).

The sample structure is as follows.
(i) For each province, a threshold is set. All municipalities with a population greater than this threshold are selected. These are auto-representative units. Below this threshold (not auto-representative units), two municipalities from each strata are chosen with probability proportional to population. From April 1995 all 1,351 municipalities are selected.
(ii) Within each selected municipality households are selected by systematic sampling from the municipal register. The sampling fraction varies from municipality to municipality in order to make the sample self-weighting within each geographical region. 75,516 households are selected in all.

The primary sample units (the municipalities) are not rotated. However, a municipality which, after a number of surveys, can no longer provide new sample households is replaced.

Rotation of the households follows a 2-2-2 rotation plan. Households are interviewed in two consecutive quarters then, after a gap of two quarters, are interviewed twice again in the same two quarters a year later.

Weighting procedure

Within each province (103), the data is post-stratified by sex, and in each region (20) by age group (0-14, 15-19, 20-29, 30-54, 55-64, 65+). The results are then adjusted to the independent population estimates.

Questionnaire

The Italian LFS is quarterly and each household participates four times. Questions concerning vocational training and situation one year ago are only put once in the Spring quarter. The other questions are identical from quarter to quarter and from wave to wave.

The questionnaire consists of:
    household questionnaire
    individual questionnaire

The household questionnaire contains, in addition to data specified by the EU codification, information for each household member on absence from the commune of residence, with reason, duration, place.

The individual questionnaire contains a number of additional questions for national purposes:
    position in occupation
    what kind of employment is sought
    permanent or temporary training contract
    in which region the person would
    accept work
    what the acceptable minimum of
    monthly earnings would be.

No complementary data from other sources are used.

LUXEMBOURG

Background

The Labour Force Survey in Luxembourg has been conducted annually since 1969.
There is no specific legislation concerning obligation to provide information for the purpose of production of the survey. Participation in the survey is voluntary.
The survey is conducted annually in the second quarter of the year and serves both national and Community purposes. It provides annual results at a national level.
The survey covers private households.
All interviews are made in a single reference week.

Sample design

The sample design consists of one stage, the sampling unit being the household.
The sampling frame is the Current Population Register.
No stratification is carried out.
A simple random sample is drawn.
25% of the sample is retained from one year to the next in order to meet EU requirements.

Weighting procedure

A post stratification is carried out by sex and age group, using independent population estimates as controls.

Questionnaire

The questionnaire consists of two parts:
    household questionnaire
    individual questionnaire.
The household questionnaire contains data (sex, age) on the reference person and an identification of the reference person. It contains the same data on the other household members and, in addition, their relation to the reference person.
The individual questionnaire is identical to the EU codification except for a single question on usual residence which is asked for national purposes.
No complementary data from other sources are used.

NEDERLAND

Background

The Dutch LFS was set up in 1973 and carried out biennially until 1985. From 1987 onwards the survey was conducted continuously throughout the whole year.
There is no specific legislation concerning obligation to provide information for the purposes of the survey. Participation in the survey is voluntary.
The survey provides annual results at national and regional level.
The survey covers only private households.
The reference weeks are spread over the whole year, with EU results being taken from the first five months of the year.

Sample design

The sample design consists of three stages:
(i) Primary sampling units are municipalities.
(ii) Secondary sampling units are addresses.
(iii) Tertiary sampling units are households.
Municipalities are selected with probability proportional to population. All municipalities with a population greater than 18,000, about 200 in all, are permanently represented.
Addresses are selected systematically from a list of addresses, which are sorted by post code. Addresses with more than one delivery, i.e. containing more than one household, are over-sampled with twice the probability of being selected.
If a selected address contains only one household, it is interviewed. If the address contains more than one household, only half the households are interviewed. This increases the efficiency of the sample by reducing clustering.
The sampling frame is a list of all addresses compiled by the Post Office. Any institutions are eliminated from the sample. The file also contains information on how many deliveries there are at each address, i.e. how many households live at the address.
65 strata are created by crossing 40 "Corop" planning regions with 28 employment exchange regions.
To meet EU requirements 25% of the respondents interviewed during the first five months of the year are re-interviewed one year later.

Weighting procedure

A two-stage post stratification is applied using independent population benchmarks.
The first stage corrects for different response rates between municipalities.
The second stage uses a linear weighting method with the constraint that every member of the household has the same weight. Three post stratifications are used:
first, a fine breakdown by region but a broad breakdown by age, sex and marital status;
secondly, a broad breakdown by region but a fine breakdown by age, sex and marital status;
finally, a broad breakdown of region by a broad breakdown of age, sex, nationality and country of birth (Dutch, Dutch nationals born in Surinam, and foreigners).

Questionnaire

Since the Dutch survey applies a different labour force definition from that recommended by ILO and adopted by the other Member States and Eurostat, the questionnaire does not put a complete range of questions to persons working less than 12 hours in the reference week. Data provided to Eurostat for the above group is produced by imputation.

The household questionnaire contains data on the number of persons in the household and demographic background data for all household members.

The individual questionnaire contains several additional items for national purposes, including:
- working hours
- disability, illness
- position or function in the job
- type of payment
- work status 3 months ago
- voluntary work
- trade union membership.

Enterprise surveys are used as a source for data on working hours.

As the interview is carried out by CAPI, many questions have alternative wording dependent on the responses to preceding questions.

ÖSTERREICH

Background

The EU LFS is carried out in the framework of the Austrian Mikrozensus, which was set up in 1967 with the purpose of establishing a current population and housing survey. It was conceived as a multi-purpose survey for different purposes within the field of social statistics. The Mikrozensus is carried out quarterly.

Legal regulations are kept to an absolute minimum. A list of subjects determines the basic questionnaire and lays down how often the survey is to be carried out. These rules give freedom to combine the basic questions with supplementary special programmes. Participation is compulsory in the basic programme, but voluntary in the supplementary special programme.

From 1995 onwards the majority of the EU LFS questions are included in the supplementary programme in the spring quarter of each year.

Private households, and communal establishments containing more than 50 persons are sampled.

The reference weeks are the three weeks at the beginning of the last month of the quarter. For any respondent the reference week is the week preceding the interview.

Sample design

The sampling unit is the dwelling. All households in the selected dwellings are sampled.

The sampling frame is based on the Census of Housing and Dwellings, updated with building records covering new dwellings.

For dwellings in the 1981 Census of Housing and Dwellings, stratification was carried out within each Länder using data taken from the census on social status and level of education of the head of household; number of occupants; age, size and facilities of dwelling. Combining these variables gives 1651 strata. The list of new buildings constructed in each year form separate annual strata.

A single stage sample is used in each stratum. The sampling ratio is 0.9% giving a sample size of some 31,000 dwellings.

A written survey is carried out within collective households. Persons with a family name beginning with the letter N are sampled.

An eight-wave rotation pattern is used. Each dwelling remains in the sample for two years, with one eighth of the sample being replaced each quarter.

Weighting procedure

A two stage process for households is used.

(i) The stratum consisting of newly constructed buildings is given greater weight. This compensates for the non-inclusion of very recently constructed buildings due to the time lag between buildings being constructed and the sampling frame being updated.

(ii) The grossed-up population is constrained to independent population estimates by Länder, sex and age band, with the further constraint that the total population of foreigners (broken down into inhabitants of Turkey, former Yugoslavia and of other countries) agrees with the latest population estimates. An iterative process is carried out which ensures that all members of a given household have the same weight.

The sample taken from collective households with more than 50 residents is grossed up to the total population in collective households.

Questionnaire

The EU Labour Force Survey is carried out within the framework of the quarterly Mikrozensus. The Mikrozensus consists of a core questionnaire ("basic programme") and varying supplementary special programmes. The core questionnaire contains a few general labour force questions and items usually asked in population and housing censuses. The core questionnaire is compulsory while the supplementary programmes are on a voluntary basis. It consists of two parts:
- household and dwelling questionnaire
- individual questionnaire

In addition to the basic programme there are special questionnaires concerning items of actual interest which change regularly. From 1995 onwards the majority of the EU LFS questions are included in the voluntary part of the survey in the first quarter of the year.

The household questionnaire contains questions on number of persons in the household and detailed information concerning housing.

The individual questionnaire contains a part of the EU LFS questions and additional questions for national purposes (school/university enrolment, economic status according to a subsistence concept).

PORTUGAL

Background

The Portuguese LFS was conducted biannually during the period 1972-1982 based on concepts and definitions identical to those employed by the Census of Population. Since 1983 the survey has been conducted quarterly on the basis of the current concepts of ILO.
Participation in the survey is compulsory, as laid down in Legislation 6/89 *Sistema Estatistico Nacional* of April 1989.
The survey produces quarterly results. Data for the purposes of the EU LFS is collected in the second quarter of the year.
The geographical territory of Portugal is covered i.e. mainland Portugal and Madeira and the Azores.
The survey covers people living in family dwellings, i.e. housing units that are usually intended to hold a single family.
The reference weeks are concentrated in a six week period in each quarter.

Sample design

The sampling units are as follows :
Primary Sampling Units are freguesias (parishes).
Secondary Sampling Units are the statistical sections used in the last census. Each statistical section contains approximately 300 dwellings.
The Tertiary Sampling Units are dwellings.
The sampling frame is the "Spatial Reference Geographical Frame" based on the results of the previous census.
The sample is stratified by the seven NUTS II regions. The sampling ratio differs between regions in order to ensure that EU requirements, in terms of sampling errors, are met.
The LFS sample is a sub-sample of the "master sample" which is used as the basis for other household surveys in Portugal as well as the LFS.
For the first stage of sampling within each region, the municipalities are arranged in a chair and the "freguesias" within the municipalities are arranged in alphabetical order. The number of electors in each freguesia is known. A systematic sample is drawn from the list of freguesias with a constant sampling interval in terms of electors. Thus freguesias with fewer electors than the sampling interval are selected with probability proportional to the number of electors within one section taken from the selected freguesias, whilst all larger freguesias are selected with the number of sections selected proportional to the number of electors.
For the second stage, within the freguesias, the statistical sections are selected with probability proportional to the number of dwellings. The selected sections form the "parent sample", which remains fixed over time.
(iii) The third stage of sampling, drawn from this parent sample, consists of sampling a number of adjacent dwellings from each section in the master sample. The number of dwellings sampled from each section is calculated so that the sample is self-weighting within regions. 22,218 dwellings are sampled in all.
A six-wave rotation plan is used with dwellings remaining in the sample for six consecutive quarters before being replaced by a similar number of dwellings from the same statistical section. One sixth of the sample is replaced each quarter.

Weighting procedure

No post-stratification is carried out. The results, corrected for differing sampling probabilities between regions, are grossed up to the total population.

Questionnaire

Data is collected quarterly with identical questionnaires. The questionnaire is divided into a household and an individual questionnaire.
As the questions have mainly yes/no responses, the number of questions are relatively large.
The household questionnaire contains status of dwelling, number of households in each dwelling, number of members in each household.
The individual questionnaire contains, besides the questions in the EU codification, a number of questions included for national purposes including the following topics:
    work in other EU countries
    wages and salaries
    frequency of wages and salaries
    how present job was obtained
    underemployment
    number of days absent from job
    type of shift work
    regular working hours
    reason for having a second job
    old age or retirement pension
    social security cover
    ability to read and write
    disability.

SUOMI / FINLAND

Background

The Finnish LFS is an independent survey, its main objective being to describe the actual situation of the labour market and furnish information about short-term trends. Participation in the survey is voluntary.
The survey has been carried out regularly every month, first as a mail inquiry since 1959. From 1983 data were collected by interviews.
From 1995 onwards data for the purposes of the EU LFS are collected in the period of March-May. Monthly results are available nationally.
Both private and collective households are sampled.
One week in each month is the reference week.

Sample design

The sampling units are individuals. The sampling frame is provided by the Current Population Register. There is a stratification by sex, by age band and region. Åland, the smallest province of Finland, is over-sampled. Otherwise the sampling fraction is constant.

A random selection is made from the current Population Register twice yearly. Each month a sample of 12,000 persons is interviewed.

For the EU LFS approximately 7,500 sampled individuals and their household members are interviewed.

Respondents are interviewed at quarterly intervals for three successive quarters then, after a six month interval, for a further two successive quarters. Retired persons aged 65 and over are only interviewed every second quarter. For the EU LFS the first waves of March to May are used.

Weighting procedure

A single-stage post stratification is used with the data constrained to the aggregates from the Current Population Register for sex, age-band and region (312 strata in all).

Questionnaire

The data is collected monthly with identical questionnaires. Up to 1994 supplementary information was collected every second year during the Autumn. From 1995 the supplementary survey has been replaced by the EU LFS in Spring. The EU LFS questions are fully integrated into the national questionnaire.

There is no household questionnaire. Data concerning the composition of the household are derived from the Central Population Register.

For the EU LFS the household is composed around the sampled individual and there are special questions about children's day care. All household members between the age of 15-74 years are interviewed.

The individual questionnaire contains some additional items for national purposes.

In the monthly survey:
- number of hours of overtime worked in the reference week
- number of days absent from work in the reference week.

In the supplementary survey:
- work experience
- unemployment (reason, duration)
- hidden unemployment
- underemployment
- part-time work (reason, duration)
- types of work schedule
- membership of trade union
- participation in training
- salary
- information about family and children

Complementary data are taken from the Central Population Register (concerning demographic background and household information) and from the register of completed education and degrees.

SVERIGE

Background

The Swedish LFS is a monthly survey with the aim of describing the current employment situation and furnishing information about labour market trends. The survey has been carried out by Statistics Sweden since 1961 with varying frequency. Since 1970 the survey is carried out monthly. From 1995 the EU LFS is carried out in April each year.

Participation in the survey is voluntary.

Reference weeks are evenly spread through the year.

Sample design

The sampling units are individuals. The Statistics Sweden Register of the Total Population (RTB) is used as the sampling frame.

The population is stratified by sex, region, nationality (Swedish/non-Swedish) and status (employed/not employed) from the Register of Employment (ARE), thus giving 192 strata.

A systematic sample from the RTB, sorted by age, is made from each strata. This results in a stratification-like effect for age. The sample is drawn at the beginning of each year, but is updated each month to take account of deaths, changes in address and marital status.

Individuals remain in the sample for two years, being interviewed eight times at three-monthly intervals. In any consecutive three month period the samples are independent. Every three months one-eighth of the sample is replaced.

Weighting procedure

When estimating the number of employed, a post-stratification for the sample and the population is carried out by sex, five year age group, employed/not employed, with control totals taken from the ARE. When estimating the number of unemployed a post-stratification is carried out by sex, age in 10 and 20 year bands and unemployed/not unemployed according to the register of the unemployed.

Questionnaire

Data are collected monthly. Solely computer assisted techniques (CATI) are used. At the first interview a thorough questioning is carried out concerning the employment situation of the sampled individual. The subsequent interviews utilise previously submitted data, which appear on the screen in the course of the interview.

UNITED KINGDOM

Background

The LFS in the UK has been conducted with varying frequency since 1973. Between 1984 and 1991 the survey was carried out annually in the March to May quarter with a sample size of approximately 65,000 households. From the March to May quarter 1992 the survey has been conducted quarterly in Great Britain with a sample size of some 60,000 households. This was supplemented by an annual survey in Northern Ireland (conducted in the Spring quarter) in 1992,1993 and 1994. From Winter 1994/1995 (December-February) the LFS is also carried out quarterly in Northern Ireland with a sample size of about 3,250.

The survey covers private households including people temporarily absent. Students living in institutions such as "halls of residence" are sampled via their parents living in private households. People living in accommodation provided by National Health Service authorities are also included.

For Great Britain the year is divided into four 13-week periods: "Winter" (December to February), "Spring" (March to May - used for EU results), "Summer" (June to August) and "Autumn" (September to November). In each quarter the reference weeks are spread evenly through the 13 weeks. For Northern Ireland, the reference weeks up to 1994 were six weeks in the middle of the "Spring" quarter. From Winter 1994/95 the reference weeks have been spread evenly over the quarter.

Sample design

The sampling unit is a postal address (in the far North of Scotland a telephone number). The sampling frame in most of Great Britain is the Postcode Address File (PAF), a database of all addresses receiving mail, compiled by the Post Office. This list is restricted to addresses receiving less than 25 pieces of mail a day in order to eliminate business addresses. Because of the very low population density in the far north of Scotland (north of the Caledonian Canal), face-to-face interviewing would be prohibitively expensive, and all interviews are carried out by telephone. In this area the telephone directory is used. In Northern Ireland, the Rating and Valuation Lists (used to administer property tax) are used. For NHS accommodation a list provided by health authorities is used. The majority of Great Britain forms one stratum, with a separate stratum for the area of Scotland where the sample is drawn from the telephone directory, and three separate strata for Northern Ireland:- Belfast, East of the Province and West of the Province. In addition the sample of NHS accommodation is drawn separately.

In Great Britain, a systematic sample is drawn from all three sampling frames using a sampling interval of 1440. This gives some 16,600 addresses from the PAF, 75 telephone numbers in the north of Scotland and 42 units of NHS accommodation. As the PAF is ordered geographically, the systematic sampling produces a pseudo-stratification effect, thus ensuring the sample is representative at a regional level. In Northern Ireland a simple random sample is drawn from each of the three strata to give 5,200 selected addresses in all. The annual sampling fraction is larger for Northern Ireland than for Great Britain (approximately 1% as compared with 0.36%), in order to give reliable results at Northern Ireland level.

A five-wave rotation scheme is used. Respondents are interviewed five times at 13 week intervals and a fifth of the sample is replaced each quarter.

Weighting procedure

A three-stage post-stratification adjustment procedure is used with the estimates being constrained to independent population estimates in each case.

(i) The stratification variable for the first stage is the "Local Authority District". This corrects for differential non-response between local authorities and ensures the results are geographically representative.

(ii) The second stage stratification variables are sex by age band (0-15, single years of age from 16 to 24 and 25+). This is designed to ensure that the age profile of the important 16 to 24 age group is correct at national level.

(iii) The third stage stratification variables are region by sex and by five year age-band.

All three stages are applied in an iterative procedure to ensure that the estimates are consistent with the sets of stratification variables.

Questionnaire

Each selected household participates in the survey in five consecutive waves. The questionnaire is identical from wave to wave, with the exception of questions on housing tenure, ethnicity and nationality, which are asked only in the first wave, and on income, only put at the last wave.

The questionnaire records household structure and housing conditions, and contains a number of questions on a wide range of topics in addition to the information included in the EU LFS, including:

- mobility (moved to find work, etc.)
- government training schemes
- PAYE scheme
- home work (extent of home use, etc.)
- travel to work
- incidence of sickness, duration
- specific working hour arrangements
- union representation
- employment 3 months ago
- benefit entitlement
- health problems ,disabilities, accidents
- income (wave 5 only).

Complementary data from other sources include claimant .(registered) unemployment data from administrative sources, and employment and earnings data from enterprise surveys.

Table 1   Sample design

	B	DK	D	GR	E	F	IRL	I	L	NL	A	P	FIN	S	UK
Collective household sampled?	yes	yes/no	yes	no	no	no	yes	no	no	no	yes	no	yes	no	yes
Frequency of results	annual	quarterly	annual	annual	quarterly	annual	annual	quarterly	annual	annual	quarterly	quarterly	monthly	monthly	quarterly
Reference week	single	evenly spread	single	multiple	evenly spread	multiple	multiple	single	single	multiple	multiple	multiple	single	evenly spread	evenly spread
Stages of sampling	2	1	1	3	2	4	2	2	1	3	1	3	1	1	1
Lowest level sample unit	Household	Person	Area	Dwelling	Dwelling	Area	Household	Household	Household	Household	Dwelling	Dwelling	Person	Person	Address
Basis of sampling frame	Register	Register	Census/Register	Census	Census	Census	Census	Register	Register	Post Office	Census	Census	Register	Register	Post Office
Stratification	Region	Unemployment	Region, size of building	Region, urbanization	Region, Urbanization Socio-economic status of area	Region, urbanization	Region, urbanization	Region, urbanization	None	Region, employment status	See text	Region	Region, sex, age band	Region, sex nationality, empl. status	None
Self weighting	no	yes	no	yes	yes within each stratum	no	no	no	yes	no	yes	no	yes	no	yes
Rotation pattern	none	3-Wave	4-Wave	4-Wave	6-Wave	3-Wave	None	2-2-2	None	None	8-Wave	6-Wave	3-1-2	8-Wave	5-Wave
Post-stratification	Age band, sex, region	Age band, sex, income, sector of activity, vocational education and registered unemployment	Sex, region, nationality	None	Age GT15 Age LE 15 Region (NUTS 3)	Age band, sex, region	Age band, sex, region	Age band, sex, region	Age band, sex	Age band, sex, region, nationality, marital status, country of birth	Age band, sex, region	None	Age band, sex, region	Age band, sex, registered employment, unemployment	Age band, sex, region

Table 2 Data collection and data processing

	B	DK	D	GR	E	F	IRL	I
Sources of information:								
- actual interview	yes	yes	yes	yes	yes	yes	yes	yes
- previous int.	no	no	no	no	yes	no	no	no
- register	no	yes	no	no	no	no	no	no
Mode of data collection:								
- face to face (paper, pencil)	yes	no	yes	yes	yes	yes	yes	yes
- face to face (CAPI)	no	no	no	no	yes from 1996	yes	no	no
- telephone (paper, pencil)	yes	no	no	no	no	no	no	no
- telephone (CATI)	no	yes	no	no	no	no	no	no
- self administ.	no	yes	yes	no	no	no	no	no
Period of data collection:								
- National LFS	May-June	Apr-June	May-June	April-July	Jan-Dec(: Aug)	March	April-May	January-April, June-October
- EU LFS	May-June	Apr-June	May-June	April-July	April-June.	March	April-May	April
Information to respondents in advance	letter	letter	letter	letter (only in Athens)	letter	letter	no	no
Field staff								
- professional	no	yes	no	yes	yes	yes	yes	no
- ad hoc	yes	no	yes	yes	no	no	yes	yes
Size of field staff	300	40	8000	450	410	1000	430	2000
Training of field staff								
- general	yes	yes	yes	no	yes	yes	yes	yes
- LFS specific	yes	yes	yes	yes	yes	yes	yes	
Response Rate								
- compulsory part	95%	--	97%	*92%-93%	-	92-93%	-	*97-99%
- voluntary part	--	77-87%	60-97%	--	*88-89%	-	95%	-
- % refusals of total non-response	15%	25-30%	-	13-18%	28-32%	32-35%	90%	15-30%
Percentage of proxy interviews	35%	3%	n.a.	49%	n.a.	30-32%	10-20%	50%
Imputation of item non-response	none	none	(NACE, working hours) +	none	yes	none	none	yes

* substitution of refusals in first wave

Table 2   Data collection and data processing

	L	NL	A	P	FIN	S	UK
Sources of information:							
- actual interview	yes	yes	yes	yes	yes	yes	yes
- previous int.	no	no	no	yes	yes	yes	yes
- register	no	no	no	no	yes	yes	no
Mode of data collection:							
- face to face (paper, pencil)	yes	no	yes	no	yes	no	no
- face to face (CAPI)	no	yes	no	yes	no	yes	yes
- telephone (paper, pencil)	no	no	no	no	yes	no	no
- telephone (CATI)	no	no	no	no	no	yes	yes
- self administ.	no	no	no	no	yes	no	no
Period of data collection:							
National LFS	April-May	Jan-Dec	March, June-Sept, Dec	Jan-Feb, April-May, July-Aug, Oct.-Nov.	Jan-Dec	Jan.-Dec.	Jan.-Dec.
- EU LFS	April-May	Jan-May	March	April-May	March-May	April	March-May
Information to respondents in advance	letter	letter	letter	letter	letter	letter	letter
Field staff							
- professional	no	yes	no	yes	yes	yes	yes
- ad hoc	yes	no	yes	no	no	no	no
Size of field staff	170	350	1200	118	155	125	500
Training of field staff							
- General	no	yes	yes	no	yes	yes	yes
- LFS specific	yes	yes	yes	yes	yes	yes	yes
Response Rate							
- compulsory part	79-85%	-	75%	91-92%	-	-	-
- voluntary part	33%	58-60%	67%	-	93-94%	86-88%	77-83%
- % refusals of total non-response		67%	25-10%	13-14%	43-47%	37-38%	65-75%
Percentage of proxy interviews	30-33%	35%	30%.	51%	8-9%.	3%	30-33%
Imputation of item non-response	none	none	none	none	(hours actually worked)	none	yes

Table 3   Implementation of the household concept

	B	DK*	D	GR	E	F	IRL	IT	L	NL	A	P	FIN	S	UK
Type of household covered:															
private	yes	yes	yes	yes	yes	yes	yes	yes	yes	yes	yes	yes	yes	yes 3)	yes
collective	yes	yes	yes	no	no	no	yes	no	no	no	yes 1)	no	yes	yes 3)	yes
Criterions for inclusion in private households:															
common dwelling	yes	yes	yes	yes	yes	yes	yes	yes	yes	yes	yes	yes	yes	yes	yes
common house keeping	yes	yes	yes	yes	no	no	yes	yes	yes	yes	yes	yes	yes	yes	yes
kinship relations	no	yes	no	no	no	no	no	yes	no	no	no	yes	no	no	no
Included:															
temporary absent persons	yes	yes	yes	yes	yes	yes	6months	yes	yes	1year	yes	3months	18months	yes	6months
persons in student homes	no	no	no	no	yes	yes	no	no	-	yes	no	yes	no	yes	yes
persons in workers homes	no	-	no	no	yes	yes	no	no	-	-	no	yes	no	no	no
domestic servants	yes	no	yes	yes	yes 2)	yes	no	no	yes	yes	yes	yes	no	no	no
lodgers	no	no	no	no	yes	no	no	no	--	no	no	no	no	no	no
conscripts	-	yes	yes	no	yes	yes	yes	no	yes	yes	yes	yes	yes	yes	-

* D-family concept
1) Collective households with 50 inhabitants or more
2) If this is the permanent dwelling of the lodger
3) The household is only covered in the EU LFS

European Union list of questions

SUMMARY
This list also shows the correspondence between column numbers of the current series and those of the series 1983 to 1991. The asterisks in the list 1983 to 1991 denote that, although there is a correspondence between the questions in the two series, some changes have been made in the conventions for coding the data.
The minimum age used to calculate the labour force has been raised from 14 to 15 years for the new series.

Column 1992	Description	Column 1983-1991
1-12	**Demographic background**	
1	Relationship to reference person in the household	17
2	Sex	18
3/4	Year of birth	19/20
5	Date of birth within the year	21
6	Marital status	22
7/8	Nationality	23/24*
9/10	Years of residence in this Member State	-
11/12	Country of birth	-
13-14	**Work status**	
13	Work status during the reference week	25
14	Reason for not having worked at all though having a job	26
15-46	**Employment characteristics of the first job**	
15	Professional status	34
16/17	Economic activity of the local unit of the establishment	35/36*
18/20	Occupation	37/38*
21/22	Number of persons working at the local unit of the establishment	-
23/24	Country of place of work	-
25/26	Region of place of work	-
27/28	Year in which person started working in current employment	-
29/30	Month in which person started working in current employment	-
31	Full-time/Part-time distinction	39
32	Permanency of the job	40
33	Total duration of temporary job or work contract of limited duration	-
34/35	Number of hours per week usually worked	28/29
36/37	Number of hours actually worked	30/31
38/39	Main reason for hours actually worked being different from person's usual hours	32/33
40	Shift work	-
41	Evening work	-
42	Night work	-
43	Saturday work	-
44	Sunday work	-
45	Working at home	-
46	Looking for another job and reasons for doing so	41
47-56	**Information about second job**	
47	Existence of more than one job or business	27
48	Professional status	-
49/50	Economic activity of the local unit of the establishment	-
51/53	Occupation	-
54/55	Number of hours actually worked	-
56	Regularity	-

Column 1992	Description	Column 1983-1991
57-68	**Previous work experience of person not in employment**	
57	Experience of employment	42*
58/59	Year in which person last worked	-
60/61	Month in which person last worked	-
62	Main reason for leaving last job	43*
63	Professional status in last job	44
64/65	Economic activity of the local unit of the establishment in which person last worked	45/46*
66/68	Occupation of last job	47/48*
69-79	**Search for employment**	
69/70	Seeking employment for person without employment during the reference week	49*
71	Type of employment sought	50
72	Duration of search for work	52*
73/74	Main method used during previous four weeks to find a job	55*
75	Date when person last contacted public employment office to find work	-
76	Willingness to work for person not seeking employment	-
77	Availability to start working within two weeks	53
78	Situation immediately before person started to seek employment (or was waiting for new job to start)	51
79	Registration at a public employment office	54
80	**Situation of inactive person**	
80	Situation of person who neither has a job nor is looking for one	56
81-87	**Education and training**	
81	Education and training received during previous four weeks	57*
82	Purpose of the training received during previous four weeks	58
83	Total length of training	-
84/85	Usual number of hours training per week	-
86	Highest completed level of general education	76*
87	Highest completed level of further education or vocational training	-
88-95	**Situation one year before survey**	
88	Situation with regard to activity	59
89	Professional status	60
90/91	Economic activity of local unit of establishment	61/62*
92/93	Country of residence	63/64*
94/95	Region of residence	65/66
96-121	**Technical items relating to the interview**	
96/97	Year of survey	1/2
98/99	Reference week	3/4
100/101	Member State	5/6*
102/103	Region of household	7/8
104	Degree of urbanisation	-
105/110	Serial number of household	9/14
111	Type of household	15
112	Type of institution	16
113	Nature of participation in the survey	67
114/119	Weighting factor	68/73
120	Sub-sample in relation to the preceding survey	74
121	Sub-sample in relation to the following survey	75

Descriptive data for main population groups

Everybody
- Demographic background (Cols. 1-12)
- Country/Region of residence one year before survey (Cols. 92-95)

Everybody aged 15 years or more
- Work status during reference week (Col. 13)
- Registration at a public employment office (Col. 79)
- Education and training received during previous four weeks (Col. 81)
- Purpose of the training received during previous four weeks (Col. 82)
- Total length of training (Col. 83)
- Usual number of hours training per week (Cols. 84/85)
- Highest completed level of general education (Col. 86)
- Highest completed level of further education or vocational training (Col. 87)
- Situation with regard to activity one year before survey (Cols. 88-91)

Persons in employment
- Reason for not having worked though having a job (Col. 14)
- Professional status (Col. 15)
- Economic activity (Cols. 16/17)
- Occupation (Cols. 18/20)
- Number of persons working (Cols. 21/22)
- Country/Region of place of work (Cols. 23-26)
- Year/Month in which person started working (Cols. 27-30)
- Full-time/Part-time distinction (Col. 31)
- Permanency of the job (Col. 32)
- Total duration of temporary job or work contract of limited duration (Col. 33)
- Number of hours per week usually worked (Cols. 34/35)
- Number of hours actually worked (Cols. 36/37)
- Main reason for hours actually worked being different from person's usual hours (Cols. 38/39)
- Shift/Evening/Night/Saturday/Sunday work (Cols. 40-44)
- Working at home (Col. 45)
- Looking for another job and reasons for doing so (Col. 46)
- Existence of more than one job or business (Col. 47)

Persons without employment
- Experience of employment (Col. 57)
- Year/Month in which person last worked (Cols. 58-61)
- Main reason for leaving last job or business (Col. 62)

If last worked less than 8 years ago:

- Professional status in last job (Col. 63)
- Economic activity of the local unit of the establishment in which person last worked (Cols. 64/65)
- Occupation of last job (Cols. 66/68)
- Seeking employment for person without employment during the reference week (Cols. 69/70)

Persons in employment and seeking another job

Unemployed persons

Inactive persons

- Type of employment sought (Col. 71)
- Duration of search for work (Col. 72)
- Main method used to find a job (Cols. 73/74)
- Availability to start working (Col. 77)

- Willingness to work for person not seeking employment (Col. 76)
- Availability to start working (Col. 77)
- Situation of person who neither has a job nor is looking for one (Col. 80)

- Date when person last contacted public employment office to find work (Col. 75)
- Situation immediately before person started to seek employment (Col. 78)

DETAILED LIST

Column	Code	Description	Filter/remarks
		DEMOGRAPHIC BACKGROUND	
1		*Relationship to reference person in the household*	private households
	1	Reference person	
	2	Spouse (or co-habiting partner) of reference person	
	3	Child of reference person (or of his/her spouse or co-habiting partner)	
	4	Ascendant relative of reference person (or of his/her spouse or co-habiting partner)	
	5	Other relative	
	6	Other	
	9	Not applicable (not private household)	
2		*Sex*	everybody
	1	Male	
	2	Female	
3/4		*Year of birth*	everybody
		The last two digits of year of birth are entered (for person 100 years old or older, supply the year 99 years ago)	
5		*Date of birth within the year*	everybody
	1	Person's birthday falls between 1 January and the end of the reference week	
	2	Person's birthday falls after the end of the reference week	
6		*Marital status*	everybody
	1	Single	
	2	Married	
	3	Widowed	
	4	Divorced or legally separated	
	blank	No answer	
7/8		*Nationality*	everybody
		For coding, see Annex IV	
9/10		*Years of residence in this Member State*	everybody
	00	Born in this Member State	
	01-10	Number of years for person who has been in this Member State for 1 to 10 years	
	11	Been in this Member State for more than 10 years	
	blank	No answer	
11/12		*Country of birth*	col.9/10≠00
		For coding, see Annex IV	
	00	Not applicable (col.9/10=00)	
	blank	No answer	

Column	Code	Description	Filter/remarks
		WORK STATUS	
13		*Work status during the reference week*	everybody aged 15 years or more
	1	Did any work for pay or profit during the reference week - **one hour or more** (including family workers but excluding conscripts on compulsory military or community service)	
	2	Was not working but had a job or business from which he/she was absent during the reference week (including family workers but excluding conscripts on compulsory military or community service)	
	3	Was not working because on lay-off	
	4	Was a conscript on compulsory military or community service	
	5	Other (15 years or more) who neither worked nor had a job or business during the reference week	
	9	Not applicable (child less than 15 years old)	
14		*Reason for not having worked at all though having a job*	col.13=2
	0	Bad weather	
	1	Slack work for technical or economic reasons	
	2	Labour dispute	
	3	School education or training	
	4	Own illness, injury or temporary disability	
	5	Maternity leave	
	6	Holidays	
	7	New job to start in the future	
	8	Other reasons (e.g. personal or family responsibilities)	
	9	Not applicable (col.13=1,3-5,9)	
	blank	No answer	
		EMPLOYMENT CHARACTERISTICS OF THE FIRST JOB	
15		*Professional status*	col.13=1,2 & col.14≠7
	1	Self-employed with employees	
	2	Self-employed without employees	
	3	Employee	
	4	Family worker	
	9	Not applicable (col.13=3-5,9 or col.14=7)	
	blank	No answer	
16/17		*Economic activity of the local unit of the establishment*	col.13=1,2 & col.14≠7
		NACE Rev. 1 For coding, see Annex II	
	00	Not applicable (col.13=3-5,9 or col.14=7)	
	blank	No answer	
18/20		*Occupation*	col.13=1,2 & col.14≠7
		ISCO-88 (COM) For coding, see Annex III	
	000	Not applicable (col.13=3-5,9 or col.14=7)	
	blank	No answer	
21/22		*Number of persons working at the local unit of the establishment*	col.15=1,3,4,blank
	01-10	Exact number of persons, if between 1 and 10	
	11	11 to 19 persons	
	12	20 to 49 persons	
	13	50 persons or more	
	14	Do not know but less than 11 persons	
	15	Do not know but more than 10 persons	
	99	Not applicable (col.15=2,9)	
	blank	No answer	

Column	Code	Description	Filter/remarks
23/24		*Country of place of work*	col.13=1,2 & col.14≠7
		For coding, see Annex IV	
	00	Not applicable (col.13=3-5,9 or col.14=7)	
	blank	No answer	
25/26		*Region of place of work*	col.13=1,2 & col.14≠7 & region within this Member State or bordering on it
		For coding, see Annex I (3rd-4th digits)	
	00	Not applicable ((col.13=3-5,9 or col.14=7), or region not in this Member State nor bordering on it)	
	blank	No answer	
27/28		*Year in which person started working in current employment*	col.13=1,2 & col.14≠7
		Enter the last 2 digits of the year concerned	
	20	Not applicable (col.13=3-5,9 or col.14=7)	
	blank	No answer	
29/30		*Month in which person started working in current employment*	col.27/28≠20,blank
	01-12	Enter the number of the month concerned	
	20	Not applicable (col.27/28=20,blank)	
	blank	No answer	
31		*Full-time / Part-time distinction*	col.13=1,2 & col.14≠7
	1	Full-time job	
		Part-time job which was taken because	
	2	- person is undergoing school education or training	
	3	- of own illness or disability	
	4	- person could not find a full-time job	
	5	- person did not want a full-time job	
	6	- of other reasons	
	7	Person with a part-time job but giving no reason	
	9	Not applicable (col.13=3-5,9, or col.14=7)	
	blank	No answer	
32		*Permanency of the job*	col.15=3
	1	Person has a permanent job or work contract of unlimited duration	
		Person has temporary job/work contract of limited duration because:	
	2	- it is a contract covering a period of training (apprentices, trainees, research assistants, etc.)	
	3	- person could not find a permanent job	
	4	- person did not want a permanent job	
	5	- no reason given	
	6	- it is a contract for a probationary period	
	9	Not applicable (col.15=1,2,4,9,blank)	
	blank	No answer	
33		*Total duration of temporary job or work contract of limited duration*	col.32=2-6
	1	Less than one month	
	2	1 to 3 months	
	3	4 to 6 months	
	4	7 to 12 months	
	5	13 to 18 months	
	6	19 to 24 months	
	7	25 to 36 months	
	8	More than 3 years	
	9	Not applicable (col.32=1,9,blank)	
	blank	No answer	

Column	Code	Description	Filter/remarks
34/35		*Number of hours per week usually worked*	col.13=1,2 & col.14≠7
	00	Usual hours cannot be given because hours worked vary considerably from week to week or from month to month	
	01-98	Number of hours usually worked in the first job	
	99	Not applicable (col.13=3-5,9 or col.14=7)	
	blank	No answer	
36/37		*Number of hours actually worked during the reference week*	col.13=1,2 & col.14≠7
	00	Person having a job or business and not having worked at all in the main activity during the reference week (col.13=2 & col.14 ≠ 7)	
	01-98	Number of hours actually worked in the first job during the reference week	
	99	Not applicable (col.13=3-5,9 or col.14=7)	
	blank	No answer	
38/39		*Main reason for hours actually worked during the reference week being different from the person's usual hours*	col.34/35=00-98 & col.36/37=01-98 & col.34/35≠col.36/37
		Person has worked **more** than usual due to	
	01	- variable hours (e.g. flexible working hours)	
	02	- other reasons	
		Person has worked **less** than usual due to:	
	03	- bad weather	
	04	- slack work for technical or economic reasons	
	05	- labour dispute	
	06	- education or training	
	07	- variable hours (e.g. flexible working hours)	
	08	- own illness, injury or temporary disability	
	09	- maternity leave	
	10	- special leave for personal or family reasons	
	11	- annual holidays	
	12	- bank holidays	
	13	- start of/change in job during reference week	
	14	- end of job without taking up a new one during reference week	
	15	- other reasons	
	97	Person having worked usual hours during the reference week (col.34/35=col.36/37=01-98)	
	98	Person whose hours vary considerably from week to week or month to month and who did not state a reason for a divergence between the actual and usual hours (col.34/35=00 & col.38/39≠01-15)	
	99	Not applicable (col.13=2-5,9 or col.34/35=blank or col.36/37= blank)	
	blank	No answer	
40		*Shift work*	col.13=1,2 & col.14≠7
	1	Person usually does shift work	
	2	Person sometimes does shift work	
	3	Person never does shift work	
	9	Not applicable (col.13=3-5,9 or col.14=7)	
	blank	No answer	
41		*Evening work*	col.13=1,2 & col.14≠7
	1	Person usually works in the evening	
	2	Person sometimes works in the evening	
	3	Person never works in the evening	
	9	Not applicable (col.13=3-5,9 or col.14=7)	
	blank	No answer	
42		*Night work*	col.13=1,2 & col.14≠7
	1	Person usually works at night	
	2	Person sometimes works at night	
	3	Person never works at night	
	9	Not applicable (col.13=3-5,9 or col.14=7)	
	blank	No answer	

Column	Code	Description	Filter/remarks
43		*Saturday work*	col.13=1,2 & col.14≠7
	1	Person usually works on Saturdays	
	2	Person sometimes works on Saturdays	
	3	Person never works on Saturdays	
	9	Not applicable (col.13=3-5,9 or col.14=7)	
	blank	No answer	
44		*Sunday work*	col.13=1,2 & col.14≠7
	1	Person usually works on Sundays	
	2	Person sometimes works on Sundays	
	3	Person never works on Sundays	
	9	Not applicable (col.13=3-5,9 or col.14=7)	
	blank	No answer	
45		*Working at home*	col.13=1,2 & col.14≠7
	1	Person usually works at home	
	2	Person sometimes works at home	
	3	Person never works at home	
	9	Not applicable (col.13=3-5,9 or col.14=7)	
	blank	No answer	
46		*Looking for another job and reasons for doing so*	col.13=1,2 & col.14≠7
	0	Person is not looking for another job	
		Person is looking for another job because	
	1	- of risk or certainty of loss or termination of present job	
	2	- actual job is considered as a transitional job	
	3	- seeking a second job	
	4	- of wish to have better working conditions (e.g. pay, working or travel time, quality of work)	
	5	- of other reasons	
	6	Person looking for another job but giving no reason	
	9	Not applicable (col.13=3-5,9 or col.14=7)	
	blank	No answer	

INFORMATION ABOUT SECOND JOB

Column	Code	Description	Filter/remarks
47		*Existence of more than one job or business*	col.13=1,2 & col.14≠7
	1	Person had only one job or business during the reference week	
	2	Person had more than one job or business during the reference week (not due to change of job or business)	
	9	Not applicable (col.13=3-5,9 or col.14=7)	
	blank	No answer	
48		*Professional status (in the second job)*	col.47=2
	1	Self-employed with employees	
	2	Self-employed without employees	
	3	Employee	
	4	Family worker	
	9	Not applicable (col.47=1,9 blank)	
	blank	No answer	
49/50		*Economic activity of the local unit of the establishment (in the second job)*	col.47=2
		NACE Rev. 1 For coding, see Annex II	
	00	Not applicable (col.47=1,9,blank)	
	blank	No answer	
51/53		*Occupation (in the second job)*	col.47=2
		ISCO-88 (COM) For coding, see Annex III	
	000	Not applicable (col.47=1,9,blank)	
	blank	No answer	

Column	Code	Description	Filter/remarks
54/55		*Number of hours actually worked during the reference week in the second job*	col.47=2
	00	Person not having worked in the second job during the reference week	
	01-98	Number of hours actually worked in the second job during the reference week	
	99	Not applicable (col.47=1,9, blank)	
	blank	No answer	
56		*Regularity of the second job*	col.47=2
	1	Second job is a regular job	
	2	Second job is an occasional job	
	3	Second job is a seasonal job	
	9	Not applicable (col.47=1,9 blank)	
	blank	No answer	

PREVIOUS WORK EXPERIENCE OF PERSON NOT IN EMPLOYMENT

Column	Code	Description	Filter/remarks
57		*Experience of employment*	col.13=3-5 or (col.13=2 & col.14=7)
	0	Person has **never** been in employment (purely occasional work, such as vacation work, compulsory military or community service are not to be considered as employment)	
	1	Person has **already** been in employment (purely occasional work, such as vacation work, compulsory military or community service are not to be considered as employment)	
	9	Not applicable (col.13=1,9 or (col.13=2 & col.14 $\neq$ 7))	
	blank	No answer	
58/59		*Year in which person last worked*	col.57=1
		Enter the last two digits of the year in which person last worked	
	09	Not applicable (col.57=0,9,blank)	
	blank	No answer	
60/61		*Month in which person last worked*	col.58/59$\neq$09,blank
	01-12	Enter the number of the month in which person last worked	
	00	Not applicable (col.58/59=09,blank)	
	blank	No answer	
62		*Main reason for leaving last job or business*	col. 57=1 and last worked < 8 years ago
	0	Dismissed or made redundant	
	1	A job of limited duration has ended	
	2	Personal or family responsibilities	
	3	Own illness or disability	
	4	Education or training	
	5	Early retirement	
	6	Normal retirement	
	7	Compulsory military or community service	
	8	Other reasons	
	9	Not applicable (col.57=0,9,blank, or col.57=1 and did not work in last 8 years)	
	blank	No answer	
63		*Professional status in last job*	col.57=1 and last worked < 8 years ago
	1	Self-employed with employees	
	2	Self-employed without employees	
	3	Employee	
	4	Family worker	
	9	Not applicable (col.57=0,9,blank, or col.57=1 and did not work in last 8 years)	
	blank	No answer	

Column	Code	Description	Filter/remarks
64/65		*Economic activity of the local unit of the establishment in which person last worked*	col.57=1 and last worked < 8 years ago
		NACE Rev. 1 For coding, see Annex II	
	00	Not applicable (col.57=0,9,blank, or col.57=1 and did not work in last 8 years)	
	blank	No answer	
66/68		*Occupation of last job*	col.57=1 and last worked < 8 years ago
		ISCO-88 (COM) For coding, see Annex III	
	000	Not applicable (col.57=0,9,blank, or col.57=1 and did not work in last 8 years)	
	blank	No answer	

SEARCH FOR EMPLOYMENT

Column	Code	Description	Filter/remarks
69/70		*Seeking employment for person without employment during the reference week*	col.13=3-5 or (col.13=2 & col.14=7)
	01	Person **is** seeking employment	
	02	Person has already found a job which will start later	
		Person **is not** seeking employment because:	
	03	- awaiting recall to work (persons on lay-off)	
	04	- of own illness or disability	
	05	- of personal or family responsibilities	
	06	- of education or training	
	07	- of retirement	
	08	- of belief that no work is available	
	09	- of other reasons	
	10	- no reason given	
	99	Not applicable (col.13=1,9 or (col.13=2 & col.14≠7))	
	blank	No answer	
71		*Type of employment sought*	col.69/70=01-02 or col.46=1-6
		The employment sought (for col.69/70=02, the employment found) is:	
	1	as self-employed	
		as employee :	
	2	- and only full-time job is looked for (or has already been found)	
	3	- and full-time job is sought, but if not available, part-time job will be accepted	
	4	- and part-time job is sought, but if not available, full-time job will be accepted	
	5	- and only part-time job is looked for (or has already been found)	
	6	- and person did not state whether full-time or part-time job is looked for (or has already been found)	
	9	Not applicable (col.13=9 or col.69/70=03-10,blank or col.46=0,blank)	
	blank	No answer	
72		*Duration of search for work*	col.69/70=01-02 or col.46=1-6
	0	Search not yet started	
	1	Less than 1 month	
	2	1-2 months	
	3	3-5 months	
	4	6-11 months	
	5	12-17 months	
	6	18-23 months	
	7	24-47 months	
	8	4 years or longer	
	9	Not applicable (col.13=9 or col.69/70=03-10,blank or col.46=0,blank)	
	blank	No answer	

Column	Code	Description	Filter/remarks
73/74		*Main method used during previous four weeks to find work*	col.69/70=01-02 or col.46=1-6
	01	Contacted public employment office to find work	
	02	Contacted private employment agency to find work	
	03	Applied to employers directly	
	04	Asked friends, relatives, trade unions, etc.	
	05	Inserted or answered advertisements in newspapers or journals	
	06	Studied advertisements in newspapers or journals	
	07	Looked for land, premises or equipment	
	08	Looked for permits, licences, financial resources	
	09	Awaiting the results of an application for a job	
	10	Waiting for a call from a public employment office	
	11	Awaiting the results of a competition for recruitment to the public sector	
	12	Other method used	
	13	No method used	
	99	Not applicable (col.13=9 or col.69/70=03-10,blank or col.46=0,blank)	
	blank	No answer	
75		*Date when person last contacted public employment office to find work*	col.69/70=01-02 & col.73/74=10
	1	At least 1 month but less than 2 months ago	
	2	At least 2 months but less than 3 months ago	
	3	At least 3 months but less than 4 months ago	
	4	At least 4 months but less than 5 months ago	
	5	At least 5 months but less than 6 months ago	
	6	6 months ago or longer	
	9	Not applicable (col.69/70≠01-02 or col.73/74≠10)	
	blank	No answer	
76		*Willingness to work for person not seeking employment*	col.69/70=03-10,blank
		Person is not seeking employment:	
	1	- but would nevertheless like to have work	
	2	- and does not want to have work	
	9	Not applicable (col.69/70=01-02,99)	
	blank	No answer	
77		*Availability to start working within two weeks*	col.69/70=01 or col.76=1,blank or col.46=1-6
		If work were found now:	
	1	Person **could start** to work immediately (within 2 weeks)	
		Person **could not start** to work immediately (within 2 weeks) because:	
	2	- he/she must complete education or training	
	3	- he/she must complete compulsory military or community service	
	4	- he/she cannot leave present employment within two weeks	
	5	- of personal or family responsibilities (including maternity)	
	6	- of own illness or incapacity	
	7	- of other reasons	
	8	- no reason given	
	9	Not applicable (col.13=9 or col.46=0,blank or col.69/70=02 or col.76=2)	
	blank	No answer	
78		*Situation immediately before person started to seek employment (or was waiting for new job to start)*	col.69/70=01-02
	1	Person was working (including apprentices, trainees)	
	2	Person was in full-time education (excluding apprentices, trainees)	
	3	Person was conscript on compulsory military or community service	
	4	Person had domestic/family responsibilities	
	5	Other (e.g. retired)	
	9	Not applicable (col.69/70=03-10,99,blank)	
	blank	No answer	

Column	Code	Description	Filter/remarks
79		*Registration at a public employment office*	everybody aged 15 years or more
	1	Person is registered at a public employment office and receives benefit or assistance	
	2	Person is registered at a public employment office but does not receive benefit or assistance	
	3	Person is not registered at a public employment office but receives benefit or assistance	
	4	Person is not registered at a public employment office and does not receive benefit or assistance	
	9	Not applicable (child less than 15 years)	
	blank	No answer	
		SITUATION OF INACTIVE PERSON	
80		*Situation of person who neither has a job nor is looking for one (excluding conscripts)*	col.69/70= 04-10, blank, & col.13≠4
	1	In education or training	
	2	Retired	
	3	Permanently disabled	
	4	Other	
	9	Not applicable (col.13=4 or col.69/70=01-03,99)	
	blank	No answer	
		EDUCATION AND TRAINING	
81		*Education and training received during previous four weeks*	everybody aged 15 years or more
	0	Received no education or training	
	1	Attended a school which provides general education	
	2	Attended a school which provides specific vocational training	
	3	Received specific vocational training in a working environment (without complementary instruction at a school or college)	
	4	Received specific vocational training within a system which provides both work experience and complementary instruction elsewhere (any form of 'dual system' including apprenticeship)	
	5	Studied for a third-level qualification which is not a university degree	
	6	Studied for university degree (initial) or recognised equivalent	
	7	Studied for a university higher degree or post-graduate qualification	
	8	Studied for some other qualification not covered above	
	9	Not applicable (child less than 15 years)	
	blank	No answer	
82		*Purpose of the training received during previous four weeks*	col.81=2-8
	1	Initial vocational training	
	2	Continuous vocational training	
	4	Other purposes	
	9	Not applicable (col.81=0,1,9,blank)	
	blank	No answer	
83		*Total length of training*	col.81=2-8
	1	Less than 1 week	
	2	1 week but less than 1 month	
	3	1 month but less than 3 months	
	4	3 months but less than 6 months	
	5	6 months but less than 1 year	
	6	1 year or longer	
	9	Not applicable (col.81=0,1,9,blank)	
	blank	No answer	

Column	Code	Description	Filter/remarks
84/85		*Usual number of hours training per week*	col.81=2-8
	01-98	Number of hours	
	99	Not applicable (col.81=0,1,9,blank)	
	blank	No answer	
86		*Highest completed level of general education at school*	everybody aged 15 years or more
	1	Less than first stage of secondary level education (that is, completed only primary education (ISCED 1) or none)	
	2	Completed first stage of secondary level education (ISCED 2) but not second stage	
	3	Completed second stage of secondary level education (ISCED 3) but not third stage	
	5	Other general education	
	9	Not applicable (child less than 15 years)	
	blank	No answer	
87		*Highest completed level of higher education or vocational training*	everybody aged 15 years or more
	1	No further education or vocational training (only general education or none at all)	
	2	Completed a course (minimum one year) at a school providing specific vocational training	
	3	Completed a course (minimum one year) of specific vocational training in a working environment (without complementary instruction at a school or college)	
	4	Completed a course of specific vocational training within a system which provided both work experience and complementary instruction elsewhere (any form of 'dual system' including apprenticeship)	
	5	Received a third-level qualification which is not a university degree	
	6	Received a university degree (initial) or recognised equivalent	
	7	Received a university higher degree or post-graduate qualification	
	8	Received some vocational qualification not covered above	
	9	Not applicable (child less than 15 years)	
	blank	No answer	

SITUATION ONE YEAR BEFORE SURVEY

Column	Code	Description	Filter/remarks
88		*Situation with regard to activity one year before survey*	everybody aged 15 years or more
	1	Person was working	
		Person was not working and:	
	2	- was seeking employment or was on lay-off	
	3	- was pupil or student in initial education or training	
	4	- was conscript on compulsory military or community service	
	5	- other	
	9	Not applicable (child less than 15 years)	
	blank	No answer	
89		*Professional status one year before survey*	col.88=1
	1	Self-employed with employees	
	2	Self-employed without employees	
	3	Employee	
	4	Family-worker	
	9	Not applicable (col.88=2-5,9 blank)	
	blank	No answer	
90/91		*Economic activity of local unit of establishment in which person was working one year before survey*	col.88=1
		NACE Rev. 1 For coding, see Annex II	
	00	Not applicable (col.88=2-5,9 blank)	
	blank	No answer	

Column	Code	Description	Filter/remarks
92/93		*Country of residence one year before survey*	everybody
	00 blank	For coding, see Annex IV Not applicable (child less than one year old) No answer	
94/95		*Region of residence (within Member State)* *one year before survey*	everybody
	00 blank	For coding, see Annex I (3rd-4th digits) Not applicable (person who has changed country of residence or child less than one year old) No answer	
		TECHNICAL ITEMS RELATING TO THE INTERVIEW	
96/97		*Year of survey* Last two digits of the year	everybody
98/99		*Reference week* Number of the week running from Monday to Sunday (except for Italy where the week runs from Sunday to Saturday).	everybody
100/101		*Member State* For coding, see Annex IV	everybody
102/103		*Region of household* For coding, see Annex I (3rd-4th digits)	everybody
104		*Degree of urbanisation*	everybody
	1 2 3	Densely-populated area Intermediate area Thinly-populated area	
105/110		*Serial number of household* Serial numbers are allocated by the national statistical institutes. Records relating to different members of the same household carry the same serial number	everybody
111		*Type of household*	everybody
	1 2 3 4 5	Person living in private household (or permanently in a hotel) and surveyed in this household Person living in an institution and surveyed in this institution Person living in an institution but surveyed in this private household Person living in another private household on the territory of the Member State but surveyed in this household of origin Person living outside the territory of the Member State	
112		*Type of institution*	col.111=2,3
	1 2 3 4 5 6 7 9 blank	Educational institution Hospital Other welfare institution Religious institution (not already included in 1-3) Workers' hostel, working quarters at building sites, student hostel, university accommodation, etc. Military establishment Other (e.g. prison) Not applicable (col.111=1,4,5) No answer	
113		*Nature of participation in the survey*	everybody aged 15 years or more
	1 2 9 blank	Direct participation Participation via another member of the household Not applicable (child less than 15 years old) No answer	

Column	Code	Description	Filter/remarks
114/119		*Weighting factor*	everybody
		Cols 114-117 contain whole numbers Cols 118-119 contain decimal places	
120		*Sub-sample in relation to preceding survey*	everybody
		This address or household :	
	1	Belongs to the sub-sample not surveyed in the previous Community labour force survey	
	2	Belongs to the sub-sample already surveyed in the previous Community labour force survey (including, where area samples are concerned, addresses of buildings constructed since the previous survey and belonging to this sub-sample)	
121		*Sub-sample in relation to the following survey*	everybody
		This address or household :	
	1	Belongs to the sub-sample not to be surveyed in the following Community labour force survey	
	2	Belongs to the sub-sample to be surveyed again in the following Community labour force survey	

ANNEX I Regional codes used in the EU Labour Force Survey
(codes according to the Nomenclature of Territorial Units
for statistics)

The following codes are used to identify the regions for which data is collected in the EU LFS.
The regional level is normally NUTS 2, except for Ireland for which NUTS level 3 is given and the
United Kingdom where NUTS level 1 is applied.

CODE	REGION	COUNTRY
BE		**BELGIQUE-BELGIE**
BE1	Rég. Bruxelles-Cap.- Brussels Hfdst. gewest	
BE2	Antwerpen	
BE22	Limburg (b)	
BE23	Oost-Vlaanderen	
BE24	Vlaams Brabant	
BE25	West-Vlaanderen	
BE31	Brabant Wallon	
BE32	Hainaut	
BE33	Liège	
BE34	Luxembourg (b)	
BE35	Namur	
DK	**Danmark**	**DANMARK**
DE		**DEUTSCHLAND**
DE11	Stuttgart	
DE12	Karlsruhe	
DE13	Freiburg	
DE14	Tübingen	
DE21	Oberbayern	
DE22	Niederbayern	
DE23	Oberplatz	
DE24	Oberfranken	
DE25	Mittelfranken	
DE26	Unterfranken	
DE27	Schwaben	
DE31	Berlin-West, Stadt	
DE32	Berlin-Ost, Stadt	
DE4	Brandenburg	
DE5	Bremen	
DE6	Hamburg	
DE71	Darmstadt	
DE72	Gieβen	
DE73	Kassel	
DE8	Mecklenburg-Vorpommern	
DE91	Braunschweig	
DE92	Hannover	
DE93	Lüneburg	
DE94	Weser-Ems	
DEA1	Düsseldorf	
DEA2	Köln	
DEA3	Münster	
DEA4	Detmold	
DEA5	Arnsberg	
DEB1	Koblenz	
DEB2	Trier	
DEB3	Rheinhessen-Pfalz	
DEC	Saarland	

CODE	REGION	COUNTRY
DED	Sachsen	
DEE1	Dessau	
DEE2	Halle	
DEE3	Magdeburg	
DEF	Schleswig-Holstein	
DEG	Thüringen	
GR		**ELLADA**
GR11	Anatoliki Makedonia, Thraki	
GR12	Kentriki Makedonia	
GR13	Dytiki Makedonia	
GR14	Thessalia	
GR21	Ipeiros	
GR22	Ionia Nisia	
GR23	Dytiki Ellada	
GR24	Sterea Ellada	
GR25	Peloponnisos	
GR3	Attiki	
GR41	Voreio Aigaio	
GR42	Notio Aigaio	
GR43	Kriti	
ES		**ESPAÑA**
ES11	Galicia	
ES12	Principado de Asturias	
ES13	Cantabria	
ES21	Pais Vasco	
ES22	Comunidad Foral de Navarra	
ES23	La Rioja	
ES24	Aragón	
ES3	Comunidad de Madrid	
ES41	Castilla y León	
ES42	Castilla-la Mancha	
ES43	Extremadura	
ES51	Cataluna	
ES52	Comunidad Valenciana	
ES53	Islas Baleares	
ES61	Andalucia	
ES62	Región de Murcia	
ES63	Ceuta y Melilla	
ES7	Canarias	
FR		**FRANCE**
FR1	Île de France	
FR21	Champagne-Ardenne	
FR22	Picardie	
FR23	Haute-Normandie	
FR24	Centre	
FR25	Basse-Normandie	
FR26	Bourgogne	
FR3	Nord - Pas-de-Calais	
FR41	Lorraine	
FR42	Alsace	
FR43	Franche-Comté	
FR51	Pays de la Loire	
FR52	Bretagne	
FR53	Poitou-Charentes	
FR61	Aquitaine	
FR62	Midi-Pyrénées	
FR63	Limousin	
FR71	Rhône-Alpes	
FR72	Auvergne	

CODE	REGION	COUNTRY
FR81	Languedoc-Roussillon	
FR82	Provence-Alpes-Côte d'Azur	
FR83	Corse	
FR91	Guadeloupe	
FR92	Martinique	
FR93	Guyane	
FR94	Réunion	
IE		**IRELAND**
IE01	Border	
IE02	Dublin	
IE03	Mid-East	
IE04	Midland	
IE05	Mid-West	
IE06	South-East (IRL)	
IE07	South-West (IRL)	
IR08	West	
IT		**ITALIA**
IT11	Piemonte	
IT12	Valle d'Aosta	
IT13	Liguria	
IT20	Lombardia	
IT31	Trentino-Alto Adige	
IT32	Veneto	
IT33	Friuli-Venezia Giulia	
IT40	Emilia-Romagna	
IT51	Toscana	
IT52	Umbria	
IT53	Marche	
IT60	Lazio	
IT70	Abruzzo	
IT81	Molise	
IT82	Campania	
IT91	Puglia	
IT92	Basilicata	
IT93	Calabria	
ITA0	Sicilia	
ITB0	Sardegna	

CODE	REGION	COUNTRY
LU (GRAND DUCHE)	**Luxembourg** (GRAND DUCHE)	**LUXEMBOURG**
NL		**NEDERLAND**
NL11	Groningen	
NL12	Friesland	
NL13	Drenthe	
NL21	Overijssel	
NL22	Gelderland	
NL23	Flevoland	
NL31	Utrecht	
NL32	Noord-Holland	
NL33	Zuid-Holland	
NL34	Zeeland	
NL41	Noord-Brabant	
NL42	Limburg (NL)	
AT		**ÖSTERREICH**
AT11	Burgenland	
AT12	Niederösterreich	
AT13	Wien	
AT21	Kärnten	
AT22	Steiermark	
AT31	Oberösterreich	
AT32	Salzburg	
AT33	Tirol	
AT34	Vorarlberg	
PT		**PORTUGAL**
PT11	Norte	
PT12	Centro (P)	
PT13	Lisboa e Vale do Tejo	
PT14	Alentejo	
PT15	Algarve	
PT2	Açores	
PT3	Madeira	
FI		**SUOMI/ FINLAND**
FI11	Uusimaa	
FI12	Etelä-Suomi	
FI13	Itä-Suomi	
FI14	Väli-Suomi	
FI15	Pohjois-Suomi	
FI2	Ahvenanmaa/Åland	
SE		**SVERIGE**
SE01	Stockholm	
SE02	Östra Mellansverige	
SE03	Småland med öarna	
SE04	Sydsverige	
SE05	Västsverige	
SE06	Norra Mellansverige	
SE07	Mellersta Norrland	
SE08	Övre Norrland	

CODE	REGION	COUNTRY

UK   **U. KINGDOM**

Code	Region
UK11	Cleveland, Durham
UK12	Cumbria
UK13	Northumberland, Tyne and Wear
UK21	Humberside
UK22	North Yorkshire
UK23	South Yorkshire
UK24	West Yorkshire
UK31	Derbyshire, Nottinghamshire
UK32	Leicestershire, Northamptonshire
UK33	Lincolnshire
UK4	East Anglia
UK51	Bedfordshire, Hertfordshire
UK52	Berkshire, Buckinghamshire, Oxfordshire
UK53	Surrey, East-West Sussex
UK54	Essex
UK55	Greater London
UK56	Hampshire, Isle of Wight
UK57	Kent
UK61	Avon, Gloucestershire, Wiltshire
UK62	Cornwall, Devon
UK63	Dorset, Somerset
UK71	Hereford & Worcester, Warwickshire
UK72	Shropshire, Staffordshire
UK73	West Midlands (County)
UK81	Cheshire
UK82	Greater Manchester
UK83	Lancashire
UK84	Merseyside
UK91	Clwyd, Dyfed, Gwynedd, Powys
UK92	Gwent, Mid-South-West Glamorgan
UKA1	Borders-Central-Fife-Lothian-Tayside
UKA2	Dumfries & Galloway, Strathclyde
UKA3	Highlands, Islands
UKA4	Grampian
UKB	Northern Ireland

ANNEX II - Statistical Classification Of Economic Activities (NACE Rev.1) - obligatory from 1993 onwards

Data is supplied at two-digit level as indicated below

Section A Agriculture, hunting and forestry

01 Agriculture, hunting and related service activities
02 Forestry, logging and related service activities

Section B Fishing

05 Fishing, operation of fish hatcheries and fish farms; service activities incidental to fishing

Section C Mining and quarrying

10 Mining of coal and lignite; extraction of peat
11 Extraction of crude petroleum and natural gas; service activities incidental to oil and gas extraction excluding surveying
12 Mining of uranium and thorium ores
13 Mining of metal ores
14 Other mining and quarrying

Section D Manufacturing

15 Manufacture of food products and beverages
16 Manufacture of tobacco products
17 Manufacture of textiles
18 Manufacture of wearing apparel; dressing and dyeing of fur
19 Tanning and dressing of leather; manufacture of luggage, handbags, saddlery, harness and footwear
20 Manufacture of wood and of products of wood and cork, except furniture; manufacture of articles of straw and plaiting materials
21 Manufacture of pulp, paper and paper products
22 Publishing, printing and reproduction of recorded media
23 Manufacture of coke, refined petroleum products and nuclear fuel
24 Manufacture of chemicals and chemical products
25 Manufacture of rubber and plastic products
26 Manufacture of other non-metallic mineral products
27 Manufacture of basic metals
28 Manufacture of fabricated metal products, except machinery and equipment
29 Manufacture of machinery and equipment n.e.c.
30 Manufacture of office machinery and computers
31 Manufacture of electrical machinery and apparatus n.e.c.
32 Manufacture of radio, television and communication equipment and apparatus
33 Manufacture of medical, precision and optical instruments, watches and clocks
34 Manufacture of motor vehicles, trailers and semi-trailers
35 Manufacture of other transport equipment
36 Manufacture of furniture; manufacturing n.e.c.
37 Recycling

Section E Electricity, gas and water supply

40 Electricity, gas, steam and hot water supply
41 Collection, purification and distribution of water

Section F Construction

45 Construction

Section G Wholesale and retail trade; repair of motor vehicles, motorcycles and personal and household goods

50 Sale, maintenance and repair of motor vehicles and motorcycles; retail sale of automotive fuel
51 Wholesale trade and commission trade, except of motor vehicles and motorcycles
52 Retail trade, except of motor vehicles and motorcycles; repair of personal and household goods

Section H Hotels and restaurants

55 Hotels and restaurants

Section I Transport, storage and communication

60 Land transport; transport via pipelines
61 Water transport
62 Air transport
63 Supporting and auxiliary transport activities; activities of travel agencies
64 Post and telecommunications

Section J Financial intermediation

65 Financial intermediation, except insurance and pension funding
66 Insurance and pension funding, except compulsory social security
67 Activities auxiliary to financial intermediation

Section K Real estate, renting and business activities

70 Real estate activities
71 Renting of machinery and equipment without operator and of personal and household goods
72 Computer and related activities
73 Research and development
74 Other business activities

Section L Public administration and defence; compulsory social security

75 Public administration and defence; compulsory social security

Section M Education

80 Education

Section N Health and social work

85 Health and social work

Section O Other community, social and personal service activities

90 Sewage and refuse disposal, sanitation and similar activities
91 Activities of membership organization n.e.c.
92 Recreational, cultural and sporting activities
93 Other service activities

Section P Private households with employed persons

95 Private households with employed persons

Section Q Extra-territorial organizations and bodies

99 Extra-territorial organizations and bodies

The breakdown by economic activity and sector used in presenting Community Labour Force Survey results corresponds to the following NACE Rev. 1 sections

Economic activity	NACE Rev. 1
Agriculture, hunting, forestry and fishing	A-B
Mining and quarrying	C
Manufacturing	D
Electricity, gas and water supply	E
Construction	F
Wholesale and retail trade, repairs	G
Hotels and restaurants	H
Transport, storage and communication	I
Financial intermediation	J
Real estate, renting and business activities	K
Public administration	L
Other services	M-Q

Sector	NACE Rev. 1
Agriculture	A-B
Industry	C-F
Services	G-Q

ANNEX III - International Standard Classification of Occupations (ISCO-88 (COM))

Data is supplied at three-digit level as indicated below

1 Legislators, senior officials and managers

11 Legislators and senior officials
111 Legislators and senior government officials
114 Senior officials of special-interest organisations

12 Corporate managers
121 Directors and chief executives
122 Production and operations managers
123 Other specialist managers

13 Managers of small enterprises
131 Managers of small enterprises

2 Professionals

21 Physical, mathematical and engineering science professionals
211 Physicists, chemists and related professionals
212 Mathematicians, statisticians and related professionals
213 Computing professionals
214 Architects, engineers and related professionals

22 Life science and health professionals
221 Life science professionals
222 Health professionals (except nursing)
223 Nursing and midwifery professionals

23 Teaching professionals
231 College, university and higher education teaching professionals
232 Secondary education teaching professionals
233 Primary and pre-primary education teaching professionals
234 Special education teaching professionals
235 Other teaching professionals

24 Other professionals
241 Business professionals
242 Legal professionals
243 Archivists, librarians and related information professionals
244 Social science and related professionals
245 Writers and creative or performing artists
246 Religious professionals
247 Public service administrative professionals

3 Technicians and associate professionals

31 Physical and engineering science associate professionals
311 Physical and engineering science technicians
312 Computer associate professionals
313 Optical and electronic equipment operators
314 Ship and aircraft controllers and technicians
315 Safety and quality inspectors

32 Life science and health associate professionals
321 Life science technicians and related associate professionals
322 Health associate professionals (except nursing)
323 Nursing and midwifery associate professionals

33 Teaching associate professionals
331 Primary education teaching associate professionals
332 Pre-primary education teaching associate professionals
333 Special education teaching associate professionals
334 Other teaching associate professionals

34 Other associate professionals
341 Finance and sales associate professionals
342 Business services agents and trade brokers
343 Administrative associate professionals
344 Customs, tax and related government associate professionals
345 Police inspectors and detectives
346 Social work associate professionals
347 Artistic, entertainment and sports associate professionals
348 Religious associate professionals

4 Clerks

41 Office clerks
411 Secretaries and keyboard-operating clerks
412 Numerical clerks
413 Material-recording and transport clerks
414 Library, mail and related clerks
419 Other office clerks

42 Customer services clerks
421 Cashiers, tellers and related clerks
422 Client information clerks

5 Service workers and shop and market sales workers

51 Personal and protective services workers
511 Travel attendants and related workers
512 Housekeeping and restaurant services workers
513 Personal care and related workers
514 Other personal services workers
516 Protective services workers

52 Models, salespersons and demonstrators
521 Fashion and other models
522 Shop, stall and market salespersons and demonstrators

6 Skilled agricultural and fishery workers

61 Skilled agricultural and fishery workers
- 611 Market gardeners and crop growers
- 612 Animal producers and related workers
- 613 Crop and animal producers
- 614 Forestry and related workers
- 615 Fishery workers, hunters and trappers

7 Craft and related trades workers

71 Extraction and building trades workers
- 711 Miners, shotfirers, stone cutters and carvers
- 712 Building frame and related trades workers
- 713 Building finishers and related trades workers
- 714 Painters, building structure cleaners and related trades workers

72 Metal, machinery and related trades workers
- 721 Metal moulders, welders, sheet-metal workers, structural-metal preparers, and related trades workers
- 722 Blacksmiths, tool-makers and related trades workers
- 723 Machinery mechanics and fitters
- 724 Electrical and electronic equipment mechanics and fitters

73 Precision, handicraft, craft printing and related trades workers
- 731 Precision workers in metal and related materials
- 732 Potters, glass-makers and related trades workers
- 733 Handicraft workers in wood, textile, leather and related materials
- 734 Craft printing and related trades workers

74 Other craft and related trades workers
- 741 Food processing and related trades workers
- 742 Wood treaters, cabinet-makers and related trades workers
- 743 Textile, garment and related trades workers
- 744 Pelt, leather and shoemaking trades workers

8 Plant and machine operators and assemblers

81 Stationary-plant and related operators
- 811 Mining and mineral-processing-plant operators
- 812 Metal-processing plant operators
- 813 Glass, ceramics and related plant operators
- 814 Wood-processing- and papermaking-plant operators
- 815 Chemical-processing-plant operators
- 816 Power-production and related plant operators
- 817 Industrial robot operators

82 Machine operators and assemblers
- 821 Metal- and mineral-products machine operators
- 822 Chemical-products machine operators
- 823 Rubber- and plastic-products machine operators
- 824 Wood-products machine operators
- 825 Printing-, binding- and paper-products machine operators
- 826 Textile-, fur- and leather-products machine operators
- 827 Food and related products machine operators
- 828 Assemblers
- 829 Other machine operators not elsewhere classified

83 Drivers and mobile plant operators
- 831 Locomotive engine drivers and related workers
- 832 Motor vehicle drivers
- 833 Agricultural and other mobile plant operators
- 834 Ships' deck crews and related workers

9 Elementary occupations

91 Sales and services elementary occupations
- 911 Street vendors and related workers
- 912 Shoe cleaning and other street services elementary occupations
- 913 Domestic and related helpers, cleaners and launderers
- 914 Building caretakers, window and related cleaners
- 915 Messengers, porters, doorkeepers and related workers
- 916 Garbage collectors and related labourers

92 Agricultural, fishery and related labourers
- 921 Agricultural, fishery and related labourers

93 Labourers in mining, construction, manufacturing and transport
- 931 Mining and construction labourers
- 932 Manufacturing labourers
- 933 Transport labourers and freight handlers

O Armed forces

01 Armed forces
- 011 Armed forces

ANNEX IV - Codification of countries

These codes are to be used for the questions on nationality (cols 7/8), country of birth (cols 11/12), country of place of work (cols 23/24), country of residence one year before the survey (cols 92/93) and Member State (cols 100/101). Countries which are given codes below should be indicated individually; in all other cases one of the general groupings should be used. Member States must be coded individually.

Code	Country	Code	Country
EU	**EUROPEAN UNION**	RA	**NORTHERN AFRICA**
BE	Belgique-Belgïe	DZ	Algeria
DK	Danmark	EG	Egypt
DE	Deutschland	LY	Libya
GR	Ellada	MA	Morocco
ES	España		Sudan
FR	France	TN	Tunisia
IE	Ireland		
IT	Italia	OA	**OTHER AFRICA**
LU	Luxembourg		Burundi
NL	Nederland		Comoros
AT	Österreich		Djibouti
PT	Portugal		Eritrea
FI	Suomi / Finland		Ethiopia
SE	Sverige		Kenya
UK	United Kingdom		Madagascar
			Malawi
EA	**OTHER EEA**		Mauritius
IS	Iceland		Seychelles
LI	Liechtenstein		Somalia
NO	Norway		Uganda
			Tanzania
			Zambia
CE	**CENTRAL AND EASTERN EUROPE**		Zimbabwe
			Angola
AL	Albania		Cameroon
	Armenia		Central African Republic
	Azerbaijan		Chad
BY	Belarus		Congo
BA	Bosnia Herzegowina		Equatorial Guinea
BG	Bulgaria		Gabon
HR	Croatia		Sao Tome and Principe
CZ	Czech Republic		Zaire
EE	Estonia		Botswana
MK	FYROM		Lesotho
	Georgia		Namibia
HU	Hungary	ZA	**South Africa**
LT	Lithuania		Swaziland
LV	Latvia		Benin
MD	Republic of Moldova		Burkina Faso
PL	Poland		Cape Verde
RO	Romania		Ivory Coast
RU	Russian Federation		Gambia
SK	Slovak Republic		Ghana
SI	Slovenia		Guinea
UA	Ukraine		Guinea-Bissau
YU	Federal Republic of Yugoslavia		Liberia
			Mali
			Mauritania
			Niger
OE	**OTHER EUROPE**		Nigeria
	Andorra		Senegal
CY	Cyprus		Sierra Leone
MT	Malta		Togo
	San Marino		
CH	Switzerland		
TR	Turkey		
	Vatican City		

NM	**NORTHERN AMERICA**	SS	**SOUTHERN AND SOUTH EASTERN ASIA**
	Bermuda		Afghanistan
CA	**Canada**		Bangladesh
	Greenland		Bhutan
	Saint Pierre and Miquelon		
US	**United States of America**	IN	**India**
			Iran
MK	**CENTRAL AMERICA AND CARRIBEAN**		Kazakhstan
			Kyrgyzstan
	Belize		Maldives
	Costa Rica		Nepal
	El Salvador	PK	**Pakistan**
	Guatemala		Sri Lanka
	Honduras		Tajikistan
MX	**Mexico**		Turkmenistan
	Nicaragua		Uzbeksitan
	Panama		Brunei
	Antigua and Barbuda	KH	**Cambodia**
	Bahamas		East Timor
	Barbados	ID	**Indonesia**
	Cuba		Laos
	Dominica		Malaysia
	Dominican Republic		Myanmar
	Grenada	PH	**Philippines**
	Haiti		Singapore
	Jamaica	TH	**Thailand**
	Netherlands Antilles	VN	**Vietnam**
	Puerto Rico		
	Trinidad and Tobago	AA	**AUSTRALIA, OCEANIA AND OTHER TERRITORIES**
LM	**SOUTH AMERICA**	AU	**Australia**
AR	**Argentina**	NZ	**New Zealand**
	Bolivia		Fiji
BR	**Brazil**		New Caledonia
	Chile		Papua New Guinea
	Colombia		Solomon Islands
	Ecuador		Vanuatu
	Guyana		Micronesia
	Paraguay		Polynesia
	Peru		
	Surinam	OT	**Other + stateless**
	Uruguay		
	Venezuela	Blank	**No answer**
EA	**EASTERN ASIA**		
CN	**China**		
	Dem. People's Republic of Korea		
JP	**Japan**		
	Mongolia		
	Republic of Korea		
	Taiwan		
WA	**WESTERN ASIA**		
	Bahrein		
IQ	**Iraq**		
IL	**Israel**		
	Jordan		
	Kuwait		
LB	**Lebanon**		
	Oman		
	Palestine		
	Qatar		
	Saudi Arabia		
	Syria		
	United Arab Emirates		
	Yemen		

ANNEX V - Attainment levels in education and training

Belgique / België

Rubrique/Kolom 86
1 Enseignement primaire ou pas d'enseignement
Lager onderwijs of geen onderwijs
2 Secondaire inférieur
Secundair onderwijs, lagere graad
3 Secondaire supérieur
Secundair onderwijs, hogere graad
4 Rubrique/Kolom 87 = 5/6/7
5 Autres
Andere

Rubrique/Kolom 87
1 Aucun enseignement ou formation complémentaire
Geen voortgezet onderwijs of beroepsopleiding
2 Formation d'**au moins un an** dans une école d'enseignement professionnel
Opleiding van minimum 1 jaar voltooid in een school voor specifieke beroepsopleiding
3 Formation professionnelle spécifique en entreprise (**un an minimum**)
Specifieke beroepsopleiding van minimum 1 jaar voltooid enkel binnen de werkomgeving
4 Formation professionnelle spécifique en alternance
Specifieke beroepsopleiding - tweeledig opleidingsstelsel
5 **Diplôme** enseignement supérieur non-universitaire
Hoger, niet universitair
6 **Diplôme** universitaire
Universitair
7 **Diplôme** post universitaire
Post-universitair
8 Autres formations postscolaires avec **diplôme**
Andere beroepsopleiding
col 87:2-3-4 : sans nécessairement l'obtention d'un diplôme ou d'un certificat

Danmark

Sajle 86
1 Folkeskole op til 8. klasse
2 Afsluttet folkeskole 9. eller 10. klassetrin
3 Afsluttet gymnasie eller Hoejere Forberedelseseksamen uddannelse
4 Sajle 87   5/6/7
5 Andet

Sajle 87
1 Ingen erhvervsuddannelse
2 Erhuerusfaglig Grunduddannelse, basisår
3 -
4 Afsluttet lærlinge- og elevuddannelse, efteruddannelse af faglærte og tillærte
5 Kortere og mellemlange videregående uddannelser af mindre end 3 års varighed
6 -
7 Mellemlange og længerevarende uddannelser af 3 års varighed eller derover
8 Anden erhvervsuddannelse

Deutschland

Spalte 86
1 Kein Hauptschulabschluß oder Realschulabschluß
2 Hauptschulabschluß / Realschulabschluß
3 Fachhochschulreife / Hochschulreife
4 Spalte 87   5/6/7
5 Andere

Spalte 87
1 Keine berufliche Ausbildung oder berufliche Schulung
2 Mittlere Reife / Hochschulreife an einer beruflichen Schule
3 Berufliches Praktikum
4 Abschluß einer beruflichen Ausbildung im dualen System (Lehre), Berufsfachschulabschluß
5 Meister- / Technikerabschluß
6 -
7 Fachhochschulabschluß / Hochschulabschluß
8 Sonstiger beruflicher Bildungsabschluß

Ellada

Column 86
1 Illiterate, Primary school or less, Dimotiko or lower
2 Gymnasio
3 General lykeio
4 Column 87   5/6/7
5 Other

Column 87
1 None
2 TCL from vocational/technical lykeio or from specialised branch of polytechnical lykeio or equivalent qualification from other institute
3 Vocational training (minimum one year) in working environment
4 TES; certificate of technical-vocational training (third-level vocational and ecclesiastic education); Technical-vocational schools (for graduates of three-year of High School)
5 Graduates with certificate of Third-level technical Education (KATEE/TEI); Graduates with certificate of SELETE/ASETEM; Graduates with certificate of Charokopios School of Home Economics
6 Graduates with certificate (Higher education)
7 Graduates with doctorate or diploma of post-doctorate studies
8 Other vocational qualification

España

Columna 86
1 Analfabetos, sin estudios, estudios primarios, ensenanza general basica (EGB), ciclos inicial y medio o primera etapa y equivalente
2 Ensenanza general: segundo grado, primer ciclo. Bachiller elemental, ensenanza general basica (EGB), ciclo superior o segunda etapa y educacion secundaria obligatoria (nuevo sistema)
3 Bachillerato superior, bachiller unificado polivalente (BUP) y bachillerato
4 Columna 87   5/6/7
5 Otra

Columna 87
1 Ninguna formación post-secundaria o profesional
2 Formación profesional de grado medio o equivalente
3 Formación profesional dentro de la empresa
4 Formación profesional mixta (en una empresa y en un centro escolar)
5 Formación profesional de grado superior o equivalente, estudios superiores no equivalentes a diplomado universitario
6 Carreras universitarias de ciclo corto; diplomados universitarios o equivalentes; tres cursos aprobados (o primer ciclo), sin derecho a titulacion, de una carrera de ciclo largo
7 Carreras universitarias de ciclo largo; Licenciados, Ingenieros, Doctores o equivalentes
8 Otra formación

France

Rubrique 86
1 Études primaires ou inférieures; 6ème, 5ème, 4ème de l'enseignement secondaire; études professionnelles sans diplôme
2 3ème, 2ème, 1ère de l'enseignement secondaire (les personnes ayant suivi un enseignement professionnel de niveau supérieur ou égal à la dernière année du Brevet d'Études Professionnelles sont supposées être passées par la classe de 3ème de l'enseignement général)
3 Terminale de l'enseignement secondaire général ou technologique, y compris préparation au brevet de technicien
4 Rubrique 87   5/6/7
5 Autres

Rubrique 87
1 Aucun diplôme supérieur ni professionnel
2 Formation professionnelle de niveau secondaire sanctionée par un diplôme (Certificat d'Éducation Professionnelle, Certificat d'Aptitude Professionnelle, Brevet d'Études Professionnelles, baccalauréat professionnel, brevet professionnel, etc.) hors apprentissage
3 -
4 Certificat d'Aptitude Professionnelle ou Brevet d'Études Professionnelles obtenu par apprentissage
5 Brevet de Technicien Supérieur, Diplôme Universitaire de Technologie, diplômes des professions de la santé (hors celle de médecin) et autres de niveau technicien supérieur
6 Licence
7 Maîtrise, diplômes universitaires du 3ème cycle (Diplôme d'Études Supérieures, Diplôme d'Études Approfondies, doctorat), Certificat d'Aptitude Professionnelle de l'Enseignement Supérieur, Certificat d'Aptitude Professionnelle de l'Enseignement Technique, agrégation; diplôme d'une grande école
8 Diplôme d'Études Universitaires Générales ou équivalent

Ireland

Column 86
1 Primary or lower
2 Junior cycle; Intermediate/Group/Junior Certificate
3 Senior cycle; Leaving Certificate
4 Column 87   5/6/7
5 Other

Column 87
1 No professional/vocational qualifications
2 -
3 At the workplace only
4 Partly within the workplace and partly at school, including apprenticeship
5 Diploma from Regional Technical College, College of Technology or equivalent
6 Bachelor degree
7 Masters or higher degree
8 Other vocational qualification

Italia

Colonna 86
1 Nessun titolo di studio; Licenza elementare; scuola media inferiore non completata
2 Licenza di scuola media inferiore; Licenza di avviamento professionale; **qualifica professionale o altro diploma di scuola media superiore che non permettete l'accesso all'universita**
3 Diploma di scuola media superiore
4 Colonna 87   5/6/7
5 Altro

Colonna 87
1 Nessuna formazione post-scolastica o professionale
2 Diploma di scuola media superiore che non permette l'accesso all'università
3 Unicamente in ambiente di lavoro
4 Apprendistato
5 Diploma universitario - Laurea breve
6 Laurea
7 Specializzazione post-laurea; Dottorato di ricerca
8 Altra formazione post-scolastica

Luxembourg

Rubrique 86
1 Niveau plus bas que secondaire inférieur
2 Niveau secondaire inférieur : CAP obtenu ou diplôme équivalent - 5 années d'études suivies avec succès dans le secondaire
3 Diplôme de niveau secondaire; 2e cycle
4 Rubrique 87   5/6/7
5 Autre enseignement général

Rubrique 87
1 Aucune formation post-scolaire ou professionnelle
2 Enseignement secondaire technique sans formation complémentaire dans une entreprise
3 Formation professionnelle spécifique au sein de l'entreprise pendant au moins une année sans autre formation complémentaire dans une école
4 Formation professionnelle spécifique dans un système de formation alternée
5 Diplôme non universitaire de niveau supérieur; enseignants du pré-primaire ou du primaire; ingénieurs-techniciens
6 Diplôme universitaire ou équivalent : études universitaires 1er et 2ème cycle; Technische Hochschule; Grande Ecole
7 Diplôme postuniversitaire: doctorat
8 Autre type de formation professionnelle

Nederland

Kolom 86
1 Al dan niet voltooid kleuter- en basisonderwijs; niet voltooid Middelbaar Algemeen Vormend Onderwijs; klas 3 Hoger Algemeen Vormend Onderwijs of Voorbereidend Wetenschappelijk Onderwijs niet met succes doorlopen (ISCED 0-1)
2 Voltooid Middelbaar Algemeen Vormend Onderwijs; klas 3 Hoger Algemeen Vormend Onderwijs of Voorbereidend Wetenschappelijk Onderwijs met succes doorlopen (ISCED 2)
3 Voltooid Hoger Algemeen Vormend Onderwijs of Voorbereidend Wetenschappelijk Onderwijs (ISCED 3)
4 Kolom 87   5/6/7
5 Overig

Kolom 87
1 Geen beroepsonderwijs of beroepsopleiding
2 Voltooid Lager Beroepsonderwijs en Middelbaar Beroepsonderwijs (ISCED 2 or 3)
3 -
4 -
5 Voltooid Hoger Beroepsonderwijs (ISCED 5)
6 Voltooide universitaire opleiding (ISCED 6-7)
7 -
8 Universitair kandidaatsexamen

Österreich

Column 86
1: Kein Pflichtschulabschluß
2: Pflichtschulabschluß
3: Lehrabschluß, Abschluß einer BMS, Matura an einer Höheren Schule, Kolleg
4: Colum 87:5/6/7
5: -

Column 87
1: Keine berufliche Ausbildung oder berufliche Schulbildung
2: Berufsbildende mittlere Schule
3: Berufspratikum
4: Abschluß einer beruflichen Ausbildung im dualen System (Lehre)
5: Berufsbildende höhere Schule
6,7 : Universitäts-, Hochschulabschluß, hochschulverwandte Lehranstalt
8: Sonstiger beruflicher Bildungsabschluß

Portugal

Coluna 86
1 Não sabe ler nem escrever; sabe ler e escrever, sem possuir o 1º ciclo do básico (antiga 4ª classe); tem **6** anos de escolaridade
2 Completou o 2º ciclo do básico (**7º, 8º e 9º anos de escolaridade**)
3 Completou o 3º ciclo do básico (**10º, 11º e 12º anos de escolaridade**)
4 Coluna 87   5/6/7
5 Outro tipo de educação geral

Coluna 87
1 Sem qualquer outro tipo de educação (apenas ensino geral ou nenhum) ou formação profissional
2 Completou um curso (mínimo de um ano) numa escola ou instituto, vocacionado para uma actividade específica
3 Completou formação específica (mínimo de um ano) num ambiente de trabalho (sem formação complementar numa escola ou instituto)
4 Completou formação específica através de um sistema com experiência de trabalho e ao mesmo tempo formação complementar noutro local (qualquer tipo de sistema "desdobrado", incluindo aprendizagem)
5 Recebeu uma qualificação de terceiro nível que não é grau universitário
6 Recebeu um grau universitário (grau de início - licenciatura ou equivalente)
7 Recebeu um grau universitário não inicial ou uma qualificação de pós-graduação (mestrado, doutoramento)
8 Recebeu uma qualquer qualificação profissional não especificada acima

Sverige

Kolumn 86
1: Förgymnasial utbildning kortare än 9 ar
2: Förgymnasial utbildning 9(10) ar; enhetsskola, grundskola
3: Gymnasial utbildning upp till 3 ar
4: Kolumn 87 5/6/7
5: Utbildning saknas samt ej hänförbar till specifik grupp
9: Ej aktuell

Kolumn 87
1: Ingen vidare yrkesutbildning
2: -
3: -
4: -
5: Eftergymnasial utbildning kortare än 3 ar (20-119 poäng)
6: Eftergymnasial utbildning 3ar eller längre (120-poäng)
7: Korskarutbildning
9: Ej aktuell

Suomi / Finland

Column 86
1: Less than primary school - Primary school or part of lower secondary or comprehensive school
2: Comprehensive school or lower secondary school
3: Matriculation examination or upper secondary school
4: Column 87:5/6/7
5: Another general education programme

Column 87
1: No vocational, professional or higher education qualification
2: Vocational or professional education in a school (minimum duration one year)
3: -
4: -
5: Vocational or professional education in a college
6: Polytechnical vocational or professional education; lower-level university degree (bachelor degree)
7: Higher-level university degree (incl. licentiate in medicine) or postgraduate (doctorate level) degree.
8: -

United Kingdom

Column 86
1 Left full-time education before 15 years of age
2 Remained in full-time education to at least 15 years of age, with or without obtaining qualifications necessary for progress to next level (e.g. 'O' level or equivalent)
3 Remained in full-time education to at least 17 years of age, with or without obtaining qualifications necessary for progress to next level (e.g. 'A' level or equivalent)
4 Column 87   5/6/7
5 Other

Column 87
1 No professional/vocational qualifications
2 Ordinary or General BTEC; RSA; City and Guilds (CGLI) or equivalent
3 -
4 Ordinary or General BTEC/SCOTBTEC, BEC/SCOTBEC, TEC/SCOTEC, SCOTVEC; ONC; OND; YTS/YT/ET
5 Higher BTEC/SCOTBTEC, BEC/SCOTBEC, TEC/SCOTEC, SCOTVEC; HNC; HND; teaching and nursing qualifications without degree
6 First degree; other degree level of qualification; graduate membership of professional institute
7 Higher degree
8 Other professional/vocational qualification

Explanatory notes to the EU list of questions

Demographic background

Col. 1 : Relationship to reference person in the household

Each private household should contain **one and only one** person coded as 'reference person', who must be an adult; this corresponds to the concept of 'head of household' previously used. Establishing the relationship between members of the household permits analysis of the data by categories of household.

Col. 5 : Date of birth within the year

Together with year of birth (Cols. 3/4) this enables the age of the respondent to be calculated. For persons born in the same year, those coded 1 (birthday falling between 1 January and the end of the reference week) will be, for the purpose of analysing survey results, effectively one year older than those persons coded 2 (birthday falling after the end of the reference week).

Col. 6 : Marital status

The status referred to here is the legal concept. It therefore does not necessarily correspond with the actual situation of the household in terms of co-habitation arrangements, as recorded in Col. 1.

Cols. 7/8 : Nationality

This should be provided according to the coding given in Annex IV. If possible the exact country should be indicated; where this is not possible, one of the general groupings in bold print should be used. Member States must be coded individually.

Cols. 9/10 : Years of residence in this Member State

For persons with up to one year's residence in this Member State, 01 should be coded; between one year and two years, 02; and so on up to 10 for persons with between nine and ten years of residence. All persons already resident for over ten years should be coded 11.

Cols. 11/12 : Country of birth

This should be provided according to the coding given in Annex IV. If possible the exact country should be indicated; where this is not possible, one of the general groupings in bold print should be used. Member States must be coded individually. For the purpose of this question, current national boundaries should be considered, rather than those existing at the time of the respondent's birth.

Work status

Col. 13 : Work status during the reference week

Information provided here, in conjunction with Col. 14, determines whether a person is considered as being in employment or not. Persons in employment are those coded 1 or 2 on Col. 13 who are not coded 7 (new job to start in the future) on Col. 14.

Code 1 : Did any work for pay or profit during the reference week

"Work" means any work for pay or profit during the reference week, even for as little as one hour. Pay includes cash payments or "payment in kind" (payment in goods or services rather than money), whether payment was received in the week the work was done or not. Also counted as working is anyone who receives wages for on-the-job training which involves the production of goods or services. Self-employed persons with a business, farm or professional practice are also considered to be working if one of the following applies :

(1) A person works in his own business, professional practice or farm for the purpose of earning a profit, even if the enterprise is failing to make a profit.

(2) A person spends time on the operation of a business, professional practice or farm even if no sales were made, no professional services were rendered, or nothing was actually produced (for example, a farmer who engages in farm maintenance activities; an architect who spends time waiting for clients in his/her office; a fisherman who repairs his boat or nets for future operations; a person who attends a convention or seminar).

(3) A person is establishing a business, farm or professional practice; this includes the buying or installing of equipment, and ordering of supplies in preparation for opening a new business.

An unpaid family worker is said to be working if the work contributes directly to a business, farm or professional practice owned or operated by a related member of the same household. Unpaid family work is any task directly contributing to the operation of the farm or family business.

Code 2 : Was not working but had a job or business from which he/she was absent during the reference week

1. *For employees*

A job exists if there is a definite and pre-scheduled arrangement between an employer and employee for regular work (that is, every week or every month), whether the work is full-time or part-time. The number of hours of work done each week or each month may vary considerably, but as long as some work is done on a regular and scheduled basis, a job is considered to exist.

Long-term absence from work. If the total absence from work (measured from the last day of work to the day on which the paid worker will return) has exceeded six months then a person is considered to have a job only if full or partial pay is received by the worker during the absence.

Seasonal workers. In some industries such as agriculture, forestry, fishing, hotels and some types of construction, there is a substantial difference in the level of employment from one season to the next. For the purpose of the labour force survey, paid workers in such industries are not considered to have a job but not be at work in off-seasons.

2. *For unpaid family workers*

The unpaid family worker can be said to have a job but not be at work if there is a definite commitment by the employer (a related household member) to accept his/her return to work.

3. *For self-employed persons*

If self-employed persons are classified as being absent from work, then they are regarded as in employment only if they can be said to have a business, farm or professional practice. This is the case if one or more of the following conditions are met:

(i) Machinery or equipment of significant value, in which the person has invested money, is used by him or his employees in conducting his business.

(ii) An office, store, farm or other place of business is maintained.

(iii) There has been some advertisement of the business or profession by listing the business in the telephone book, displaying a sign, distributing cards or leaflets, etc.

If none of these conditions is met, then the person is regarded as not being in employment.

Code 3 : Was not working because on lay-off

A person on lay-off is one whose written or unwritten contract of employment, or activity, has been suspended by the employer for a specified or unspecified period at the end of which the person concerned has a recognised right or recognised expectation to recover employment with that employer.

Col 14 : Reason for not having worked at all though having a job

This item is addressed to those persons who had a job but did not work at all during the reference week (Filter: Col.13=2).

Code 1 : Slack work for technical or economic reasons

This includes difficulties such as plant breakdown or materials shortage; see also note below on Code 2.

Code 2 : Labour dispute

This code only applies to persons who were directly involved in a labour dispute. Other persons who did not work because production in the establishment was impeded by a labour dispute outside the establishment (thus causing a shortage in material supplies for example) are coded 1 : "slack work for technical or economic reasons".

Code 5 : Maternity leave

This code is used only for those persons on statutory maternity leave. Any other leave taken for reasons of child-bearing or rearing is coded 8 : "Other reasons".

Code 7 : New job to start in the future

This code identifies those persons who on Col. 13 are classified as having a job in the reference week and not having worked, who in effect have found a job which has not yet started. These persons are regarded as unemployed. There may also be other persons in essentially the same situation who on Col. 13 are classified as not having a job in the reference week and declare under Col. 69/70 that they have found a job which will start later. These persons are also regarded as unemployed.

Employment characteristics of the first job

Definition of the first job

For the purposes of Cols. 15 to 45, multiple job holders decide for themselves which job is to be considered as the first job. In doubtful cases the first job should be the one with the greatest number of hours usually worked. Persons having changed job during the reference week should regard the job held at the end of the reference week as their first job.

Col. 15 : Professional status

Code 1 : Self-employed with employees

Self-employed persons with employees are defined as persons who work in their own business, professional practice or farm for the purpose of earning a profit, and who employ at least one other person.

Code 2 : Self-employed without employees

Self-employed persons without employees are defined as persons who work in their own business, professional practice or farm for the purpose of earning a profit, and who do not employ any other person.

Code 3 : Employee

Employees are defined as persons who work for a public or private employer and who receive compensation in the form of wages, salaries, fees, gratuities, payment by results or payment in kind; non-conscript members of the armed forces are also included.

Code 4 : Family worker

Family workers are persons who help another member of the family to run an agricultural holding or other business, provided they are not considered as employees.

Cols. 16/17 : Economic activity of the local unit of the establishment

The NACE codes in Annex II are derived from the Statistical Classification of Economic Activities (NACE Rev. 1)

By "establishment" is meant a business, professional practice, farm, enterprise, manufacturer, public corporation, etc. The "local unit" to be considered is the geographical location where the job is mainly carried out or, in the case of peripatetic occupations, can be said to be based; normally it consists of a single building, part of a building, or, at the largest, a self-contained group of buildings. The "local unit of the establishment" is therefore the group of employees of the enterprise who are geographically located at the same site.

Cols. 18/20 : Occupation

This should be coded according to the ISCO-88 (COM) classification provided in Annex III, which is based upon *ISCO-88; International Standard Classification of Occupations,* published by the International Labour Office (Geneva, 1990).

Cols. 21/22 : Number of persons working at the local unit of the establishment

For the term "local unit of the establishment", see notes to Cols. 16/17. The codes provided permit either a reasonably exact number to be indicated (codes 01-13) or simply an indication of whether it is greater or less than ten (codes 14 and 15).

Cols. 23/24 : Country of place of work

This should be provided according to the coding shown in Annex IV. If possible the exact country should be indicated; where this is not possible, one of the general groupings in bold print should be used. Member States must be coded individually.

Cols. 25/26 : Region of place of work

This should be provided to the coding system in Annex I, which is based upon the Nomenclature of Territorial Units (NUTS). The third and fourth digits of the NUTS code (that is, the level II regional code) should be provided. This information should be supplied if the person works within the Member State where he or she lives. If the person works in a different Member State, it is required only in those cases where the person works in a region bordering on the Member State where he or she lives.

Cols. 27/28 and 29/30: Year/Month in which the person started working for this employer or as self-employed

This information is valuable for estimating the degree of fluidity in the labour market and in identifying the areas of economic activity where the turnover of labour is rapid or otherwise. The exact date of starting a job is so often required that most respondents can supply the month without difficulty, and in almost all cases if the job was begun within the last year.

Col. 31 : Full-time / part-time distinction

The distinction between full-time and part-time work should be made on the basis of a spontaneous answer given by the respondent. It is impossible to establish a more exact distinction between part-time and full-time work, due to variations in working hours between Member States and also between branches of industry. By checking the answer with the number of hours usually worked, it should be possible to detect and even to correct improbable answers, since part-time work will hardly ever exceed 35 hours, while full-time work will usually start at about 30 hours.

Codes 2 to 6 are in order of priority with code 2 having the highest priority. Code 7 identifies those persons who declare they work part-time but give no reason.

Col. 32 : Permanency of the job

This question is addressed **only to employees.**

In the majority of Member States most jobs are based on written work contracts. However in some countries such contracts exist only for specific cases (for example in the public sector, for apprentices, or for other persons undergoing some formal training within an enterprise). Taking account of these different institutional arrangements the notions "temporary job" and "work contract of limited duration" (likewise "permanent job" and "work contract of unlimited duration") describe situations which under different institutional frameworks, can be regarded as similar.

A job may be regarded as temporary if it is understood by both employer and the employee that the termination of the job is determined by objective conditions such as reaching a certain date, completion of an assignment or return of another employee who has been temporarily replaced. In the case of a work contract of limited duration the condition for its termination is generally mentioned in the contract.

To be included in these groups are :

(i) persons with a seasonal job,

(ii) persons engaged by an employment agency or business and hired out to a third party for the carrying out of a "work mission" (unless there is a work contract of unlimited duration with the employment agency or business),

(iii) persons with specific training contracts.

If there exists no objective criterion for the termination of a job or work contract these should be regarded as permanent or of unlimited duration (Code 1).

Code 6 : Contract for a probationary period

This code applies only if a contract finishes automatically at the end of the probationary period, necessitating a new contract if the person continues to be employed by the same employer.

Col. 33 : Total duration of temporary job or work contract of limited duration

This refers to the total of the time already elapsed and the time remaining until the end of the contract.

Cols. 34/35 : Number of hours per week usually worked

The number of hours given here corresponds to the number of hours the person normally works. This covers all hours including extra hours, either paid or unpaid, which the person normally works, but excludes the travel time between the home and the place of work as well as the main meal breaks (normally taken at midday). Persons who usually also work at home (within the definitions given in the notes to Col. 45) are asked to include the number of hours they usually work at home. Apprentices, trainees and other persons in vocational training are asked to exclude the time spent in school or other special training centres.

Some persons, particularly the self-employed and family workers, may not have usual hours, in the sense that their hours vary considerably from week to week or month to month. When the respondent is unable to provide a figure for usual hours for this reason, the average of the hours actually worked per week over the past four weeks is used as a measure of usual hours.

Code '00' is applied to those cases where neither the number of usual hours nor an average number of hours worked over the past four weeks can be established.

Cols. 36/37 Number of hours actually worked during the reference week

The number of hours given here corresponds to the number of hours the person actually worked during the reference week. This includes all hours including extra hours regardless of whether they were paid or not. Travel time between home and the place of work as well as the main meal breaks (normally taken at midday) are excluded. Persons who have also worked at home (within the definitions given in the notes to Col. 45) are asked to include the number of hours they have worked at home. Apprentices, trainees and other persons in vocational training are asked to exclude the time spent in school or other special training centres.

Cols. 38/39 : Main reason for hours actually worked during the reference week being different from the person's usual hours

This question should also be asked of those persons who did not state their usual hours (Cols. 34/35 = 00). They may know if they have worked considerably more or less than usual even if they cannot give a number for their usual hours.

In a case where more than one reason applies, the reason to be coded is that which explains the greatest number of hours.

Code 04 : Slack work for technical or economic reasons

This includes difficulties such as plant breakdown or materials shortage; see also note below on Code 05.

Code 05 : Labour dispute

This code only applies to persons who were directly involved in a labour dispute. Other persons who did not work because production in the establishment was impeded by a labour dispute (thus causing a shortage in material supplies, for example) are coded 04.

Code 09 : Maternity leave

This code is used only for those persons who were on statutory maternity leave. Any other leave taken for reasons of child-bearing or rearing is coded 10 : "special leave for personal or family reasons".

Col. 40 : Shift work

The question on shift work is addressed only to employees. Work shifts are defined as two or more distinct periods of work within a 24-hour day between which employees are regularly rotated. An employee is therefore classified as shift worker if he/she works two or more different work shifts. Persons working fixed hours (i.e whose working hours do not vary significantly) are not considered as shift workers. For example, a person who always works the night "shift"in a factory, should be coded with 3 in this column and 1 in Col. 42.

Code 1 : Person usually does shift work

"Usually" in this context may be interpreted to mean that the times at which a person worked varied significantly more than once during a reference period of four weeks preceding the interview.

Code 2 : Person sometimes does shift work

"Sometimes" in this context may be interpreted to mean that the times at which the person worked varied significantly once (but not more often) during a reference period of four weeks preceding the interview.

Code 3 : Person never does shift work

"Never" in this context may be interpreted to mean that the times at which the person worked did not vary significantly during a reference period of four weeks preceding the interview.

Col. 41 : Evening work

The definitions of evening and night vary considerably so that it is not easy to establish a strictly common basis for all Member States. Generally speaking, however, "evening work" can be considered to be work done after the usual hours of working time in this Member State, but before the usual sleeping hours. This implies the possibility of sleeping at normal times (whereas"night work" implies an abnormal sleeping pattern).

Code 1 : Person usually works in the evening

"Usually" in this context may be interpreted to mean on at least half of the days worked in a reference period of four weeks preceding the interview.

Code 2 : Person sometimes works in the evening

"Sometimes" in this context may be interpreted to mean on less than half of the days worked (but on at least one occasion) in a reference period of four weeks preceding the interview.

Code 3 : Person never works in the evening

"Never" in this context may be interpreted to mean on no occasion in a reference period of four weeks preceding the interview.

Col. 42 : Night work

Bearing in mind the definitional problems discussed under Col. 41, "night work" can be generally be considered to be work done during the usual sleeping hours. This implies an abnormal sleeping pattern (whereas "evening work" implies the possibility of sleeping at normal times).

Code 1 : Person usually works at night

"Usually" in this context may be interpreted to mean on at least half of the days worked in a reference period of four weeks preceding the interview.

Code 2 : Person sometimes works at night

"Sometimes" in this context may be interpreted to mean on less than half of the days worked (but on at least one occasion) in a reference period of four weeks preceding the interview.

Code 3 : Person never works at night

"Never" in this context may be interpreted to mean on no occasion in a reference period of four weeks preceding the interview.

Col. 43 : Saturday work

This should be strictly interpreted in terms of formal working arrangements. Thus employees who, on their own initiative, take some of their work home or work at the place of business on Saturdays should not be included in this classification, even if they have done so during the reference period of four weeks preceding the interview.

Code 1 : Person usually works on Saturdays

"Usually" in this context may be interpreted to mean on two or more Saturdays in a reference period of four weeks preceding the interview.

Code 2 : Person sometimes works on Saturdays

"Sometimes" in this context may be interpreted to mean on one Saturday in a reference period of four weeks preceding the interview.

Code 3 : Person never works on Saturdays

"Never" in this context may be interpreted to mean not on any Saturday in a reference period of four weeks preceding the interview.

Col. 44 : Sunday work

This should be strictly interpreted in terms of formal working arrangements. Employees who take some of their office work home and/or work occasionally at the place of business on Sundays should not be included in this classification.

Code 1 : Person usually works on Sundays

"Usually" in this context may be interpreted to mean on two or more Sundays in a reference period of four weeks preceding the interview.

Code 2 : Person sometimes works on Sundays

"Sometimes" in this context may be interpreted to mean on one Sunday in a reference period of four weeks preceding the interview.

Code 3 : Person never works on Sundays

"Never" in this context may be interpreted to mean not on any Sunday in a reference period of four weeks preceding the interview.

Col. 45 : Working at home

This concept applies to many self-employed people, for example in artistic or professional activities, who work wholly or partly at home, often in a part of their living accommodation set aside for this purpose. However, if the place of work comprises a separate unit (for example, a doctor's surgery or tax consultant's practice) which is adjacent to the person's home but contains a separate entrance, then work performed there should not be considered to be done "at home". Similarly, a farmer is not to be regarded as working "at home" when he is occupied in fields or buildings adjacent to his house.

In the case of employees, "working at home" should be interpreted strictly in terms of formal working arrangements, where it is mutually understood by the employee and the employer that a certain part of the work is to be done at home. Such an arrangement may be explicitly included in the terms of employment, or may be recognised in other ways (for example, if the employee explicitly notifies the employer of this work by completing a timesheet, or by requesting additional payment or other forms of compensation). This arrangement is also recognised if an employee is equipped with a computer in his home in order to perform his work. Other typical examples of "working at home" include travelling salesmen who prepare at home for appointments with clients which are then held at the clients' offices or homes, or persons who do typing or knitting work which on completion is sent to a central location.

"Working at home" does not cover cases where employees carry out tasks at home (because of personal interest or pressure of time), which under their working arrangements might equally have been performed at their place of work.

Code 1 : Person usually works at home

"Usually" in this context may be interpreted to mean that during a reference period of four weeks preceding the interview, the person did work at home within the framework of an agreement as described above, and the number of occasions on which he did so amounted to half or more of the days worked in this period.

Code 2 : Person sometimes works at home

"Sometimes" in this context may be interpreted to mean that during a reference period of four weeks preceding the interview, the person did work at home within the framework of an agreement as described above, but the number of occasions on which he did so amounted to less than half of the days worked in this period.

Code 3 : Person never works at home

"Never" in this context may be interpreted to mean that during a reference period of four weeks preceding the interview, the person did not on any occasion work at home within the framework of an agreement as described above.

Col. 46 : Looking for another job and reasons for doing so

Codes 1 - 5 are in order of priority with code 1 having the highest priority. Code 6 identifies those persons who declare they are looking for another job but give no reason.

Information about second jobs

Col. 47 : Existence of more than one job or business

Code 2 : Person had more than one job or business during the reference week

This refers only to those persons with more than one job. It does not refer to persons having changed job during the reference week.

Col. 48 : Professional status in the second job

See notes to Col. 15.

Cols. 49/50 : Economic activity of the local unit of the establishment of the second job

The NACE codes in Annex II are derived from the Statistical Classification of Economic Activities (NACE Rev. 1). For the term "local unit of the establishment" see notes to Cols. 16/17.

Cols. 51/53 : Occupation in the second job

This should be coded according to the ISCO-88 (COM) classification provided in Annex III, which is based upon *ISCO-88; International Standard Classification of Occupations,* published by the International Labour Office (Geneva, 1990).

Previous work experience of person not in employment

Col. 57 : Experience of employment

This column is used to define whether a person without employment has previously been in employment and, if so, Cols. 58/59 & 60/61 provide information on the month and year in which he/she last worked.

Although compulsory military or community service is not regarded as employment in the framework of the survey, respondents who, after having left their last job were conscripts on compulsory military or community service should indicate the month and year in which they completed this service.

Cols. 58/59 and 60/61: Year/Month in which person last worked

The information on the year and month when the person last worked permits an exact calculation to be made of the length of time which has elapsed since the person was in employment. In the case of unemployed persons, this is used in the estimation of the duration of unemployment, which is defined as the shorter of the following two periods : the length of time since last employment and the duration of search for work (Col. 72).

Col. 62 : Main reason for leaving last job or business

Code 0 : Dismissed or made redundant

This code is used for employees whose employment ended involuntarily. It includes those employees who were dismissed, made redundant, or lost their job because their employer either went out of business, sold or closed down the business.

Code 1 : A job of limited duration has ended

This code is used for employees who declare that their last job was temporary and came to an end, or that they had a formal work contract which was completed. This also applies to seasonal and casual jobs.

Code 2 : Personal or family responsibilities

Personal or family responsibilities may include marriage, pregnancy, childcare, serious illness of another member of the family, long vacation etc. However, if the respondent left his/her job because of personal health-related reasons then code 3 should be used.

Code 5 : Early retirement

This code applies mainly to those employees who have taken the early retirement option due to economic factors (labour market problems, difficulties in specific sectors of the economy, etc.). If the respondent retired from his/her job at the normal retirement age then code 6 should be used.

Code 8 : Other reasons

This code is used where none of the codes 0-7 applies, including cases where the person has resigned from his job for reasons (such as personal dissatisfaction) not covered by any of the other codes.

Col. 63 : Professional status in the last job

See notes to Col. 15.

Cols. 64/65 : Economic activity of the local unit of the establishment in which person last worked

The NACE codes in Annex II are derived from the Statistical Classification of Economic Activities (NACE Rev. 1). For the term "local unit of the establishment", see notes to Cols. 16/17.

Cols. 66/68 : Occupation of last job

This should be coded according to the ISCO-88 (COM) classification provided in Annex III, which is based upon *ISCO-88; International Standard Classification of Occupations,* published by the International Labour Office (Geneva, 1990).

Search for employment

Cols. 69/70 : Seeking employment for person without employment during the reference week

Due to the importance of this question in defining the unemployed, every effort should be made to ensure that an answer is given to this question. 'Blanks' should be kept to a minimum.

Those people not seeking employment (i.e. codes 03 to 10 or blank) are questioned on their willingness to work on Col. 76.

Code 01 : Person is seeking employment

Also considered as seeking employment is a person who seeks an opportunity of professional training within an enterprise, e.g. as an apprentice or trainee.

Code 02 : Person has already found a job which will start later

As mentioned in the notes to Col. 14 code 7, this applies to all persons without a job during the reference week who have already found a job which will start later. This information is sufficient to classify them as unemployed.

Code 03 : Awaiting recall to work (persons on lay-off)

This code is to re-identify those persons who on Col. 13 declare to be on lay-off and not seeking employment.

Code 08 : Belief that no work is available

This code permits the estimation of the number of unemployed according to the ILO extended definition of unemployment.

Col. 71 : Type of employment sought

Code 1 : As self-employed

Persons seeking self-employment, who are without employment during the reference week, are also asked under Cols. 73/74 whether they have taken any active steps during the past 4 weeks to set up a business, farm or professional practice.

Codes 2/5 : Only full-time/part time job is looked for (or has already been found)

Persons having already found a job as employee which will start later should be coded either 2 or 5 depending on whether the job found is a full-time or a part-time job. Codes 3 and 4 do not apply for this group.

Col. 72 : Duration of search for work

In the case of unemployed persons, this is used in the estimation of the duration of unemployment, which is defined as the shorter of the following two periods : the length of time since last employment (see notes on Cols. 58-61) and the duration of search for work.

Cols. 73/74 : Main method used during previous four weeks to find work

Due to the importance of this column for the classification of the unemployed the different answers should be prompted. Only those methods used during the four weeks before the interview are to be recorded.

Code 10 : Waiting for a call from a public employment office

This code is not to be used in the case of persons who have taken the initiative in making contact with the public employment office during the last four weeks (in this case the code to be used is '01'). It is to be used only for those persons who have not undertaken any more active step during the four-week reference period than waiting for a call from a public employment office; this implies that contact with the public employment office was established at some point before the reference period. Column 75 establishes the date at which this contact was last made.

Code 11 : Awaiting the results of a competition for recruitment to the public sector

In general, the fact of awaiting the results of an application or competition alone does not indicate a strong enough attachment to the labour market to justify classifying a person in this situation as unemployed. An exception is made in the case of a competition for recruitment in the public sector because for persons with specific qualifications this may be the only employer to offer suitable jobs (e.g. as teachers, policemen) and competitions may be the only way to enter this sector.

Col. 75 : Date when person last contacted employment office to find work

This column is intended to measure the period since the last active step was taken to find work, by those persons not declaring any other search method than "waiting for a call from a public employment office" (Cols. 73/74 = 10). It permits a calculation to be made corresponding to those (non-ILO) definitions of unemployment which do not include the criterion of active job-search within the past four weeks.

Col. 76 : Willingness to work for person not seeking employment.

This question is intended to permit a more exact measure for "discouraged workers". It is put to persons coded 03-10 on Cols. 69/70, i.e. without employment and not seeking employment.

Col. 77 : Availability to start working within next two weeks

Persons seeking paid employment must be immediately available for work in order to be considered unemployed. 'Immediately available' means that if a job were found at the time of the interview, the person would be able to start work within two weeks. Testing for availability in the two weeks after the interview is considered more appropriate than testing during the reference week, because some persons may be unavailable for work during the reference week due to obstacles that might have been overcome had they known that a job was available to them. In order to obtain a wider view of the movement of the labour market, this question is also put to persons in employment who are looking for another job (Col. 46 = 1-6) and to "discouraged workers" (Col. 76 = 1).

Col. 78 : Situation immediately before person started to seek employment (or was waiting for new job to start)

This information permits a distinction to be made between categories of unemployed persons, namely job-losers/leavers, entrants and re-entrants. Job-losers/leavers are persons who were working before seeking work (Code 1), while entrants and re-entrants were outside the labour force (Codes 2 to 5).

Col. 79 : Registration at a public employment office

This question is to be answered by everybody of working age participating in the survey. For persons having declared themselves to be seeking employment this question should be the last in the section on seeking employment, as it is important not to give the subject of registration too much emphasis in defining the unemployed. Since unemployment will basically be defined by the criteria of job search and availability for work the respondents' answer to these questions should not be conditioned by whether or not they are registered at an official employment exchange. It is expected that by following this rule the comparability of unemployment figures will be improved.

Persons not seeking employment are also asked this question. By putting this question to everybody it should be possible to better compare the unemployment figures derived from the survey with those from the unemployment registers.

Situation of inactive person

Col. 80 : Situation of person who neither has a job nor is looking for one (excluding conscripts)

Code 3 : Permanently disabled

This code should only be used when a person believes that he/she would be unable to work regardless of what jobs become available.

Education and training

Col. 81 : Education and training received during previous four weeks

This question provides basic information on education and training currently being received. The question is addressed to all persons aged 15 or older, this being the minimum for compulsory education in all Member States. A reference period of four weeks is proposed in order to reduce the risk that the week preceding the interview coincided with a vacation or other interval in the education or training.

The information collected here should relate only to education and vocational training which is relevant for the current or possible future job of the respondent. Courses undertaken purely for interest or as hobbies should not be included. Instruction with a general application, such as driving lessons, should also be excluded, unless undertaken with the specific intention of seeking a job in which this was indispensable.

If during the past four weeks education or vocational training was received in more than one institution, the training which is considered the most important by the respondent should be coded; in doubtful cases this is the course of training which has occupied the greatest number of hours during the past four weeks. However, as an exception to this rule, persons following a training programme in the dual system which involves both school and establishment (e.g. apprenticeship, sandwich courses) should always be coded '4'.

The various possible codes for this column, as discussed below, have been designed to correspond as exactly as possible to those offered in Col. 87. The notes provided for that column may therefore supply useful supplementary guidance.

Code 0 : Received no education or training

For many persons with jobs, but not all, this will be the appropriate code. Employees who have been sent on short courses in, for example, computer usage, should be coded 3, while other persons who may be studying in their free time for Open University degrees or other courses, possibly by correspondence, should be coded '6'.

Code 1 : Attended a school which provides general education

This code identifies schools of the type attended up to the age of 15, and it will therefore be the appropriate code for many people just over that age, who are not yet receiving training intended to provide qualifications for a specific vocation.

Code 2 : Attended a school which provides specific vocational training

This will be the appropriate code for many persons who are intending to take up a skilled manual occupation and are receiving the necessary instruction at an educational or training institution. If, however, the instruction is categorised as "third-level" (that is to say it follows after a complete course of secondary level education) it will probably qualify for codes '5', '6' or '7', which should be used in this case.

Code 3 : Received specific vocational training in a working environment (without complementary instruction at a school or college)

This refers to vocational training either received at the place of work or else made available or paid for by the person's employer. If the vocational training in the working environment was received within the context of the so-called "dual system", then even if during the past four weeks the training took place entirely in the working environment the code to be used is not '3' but '4'.

Code 4 : Received specific vocational training within a system which provides both work experience and complementary instruction elsewhere (any form of "dual system" including apprenticeship)

For this code to be the appropriate one, the training and practical elements must be explicitly integrated into a single system. As discussed above, persons attending training programmes in a "dual system" are to be coded '4' even if the training received during the past four weeks was entirely within a working environment or entirely in a school.

Code 5 : Studied for a third-level qualification which is not a university degree

Study for a "third level" qualification implies that the person has completed general education up to the end of second level. If this is the case code '5' should be used unless the qualification sought is a university degree. Examples of code '5' include diplomas in teaching and nursing.

Code 6 : Studied for a university degree (initial) or equivalent

This is the appropriate code for study at university level unless the person has already obtained a degree and is now seeking a further qualification (which would be coded '7').

Code 7 : Studied for a university higher degree or post-graduate qualification

In this case again the study must be at university level. The qualification sought will normally be a doctorate or master's degree.

Code 8 : Studied for some other qualification not covered above

This code has been introduced to cover types of education and vocational training which are difficult to classify within the scheme outlined above.

Col. 82 : Purpose of the training received during previous four weeks

This question is put to all persons of 15 or over (the most common limit for compulsory education) who were receiving education or vocational training during the previous four weeks (Filter : Col. 81 = 2-8). The code to be used is determined largely by the declared intentions of the person receiving the training.

Code 1 : Initial vocational training

This code applies to all persons undergoing education or vocational training who have never worked (except purely occasional work, compulsory military or alternative community service).

Code 2 : Advancement in career

This code refers to all persons who, in the reference week, were receiving training to improve their qualifications in their present occupation.

Code 3 : Changing career

This code refers to all persons who, in the reference week, were receiving training in an area different from their present or previous occupation, with a view to changing jobs This may also include persons who have a recognised vocational qualification but no relevant work experience, provided the subject area of the present training is substantially different from the training already completed.

Col. 83 : Total length of training

This question refers only to the course of training identified in Col. 81. It is the total length of the period already completed in this course, plus the period which the person is obliged to complete. It does not take into account earlier courses which led to a separate qualification or diploma, nor succeeding courses which the person may intend to take but which do not form an intrinsic part of the same training. The concept is one of elapsed time, so no adjustment is to be made in the case of courses which are not full-time. This is taken into account in the following question.

Col. 84/85 : Usual number of hours training per week

This question refers only to the course of training identified in Col. 81. The week to be considered should be a typical one, bearing in mind the four-week reference period, and thus excluding untypical periods such as vacations.

Col. 86 and col. 87

These two questions provide information on the educational and training attainment of respondents. They are addressed to all persons aged 15 years or more.

These questions cover respectively the "highest completed level of general education" (column 86) and "the highest completed level of further education or vocational training" (column 87). This implies an agreed set of conventions distinguishing between general education on the one hand and vocational education on the other. They are based on the following widely accepted principles.

All current programmes at primary education are regarded as general education: most programmes at secondary level can be coded unambiguously but a small number might be coded either way. Programmes offering a range of subjects in humanities, mathematics, natural science, social science, technology and creative arts from which a student can choose, which are designed to facilitate further study at the next level are regarded as general, e.g. most programmes provided at junior second level are readily classified as general education. Those which are tailored to preparation for a specific occupation or profession and are either terminal or intended to facilitate further study only within the ambit of further preparation towards the same occupation are regarded as vocational training, e.g. a programme leading to a qualification as a plumber, as are programs designed for those in a particular occupation with the intention of improving or updating skills in that occupation. There are some programmes which are not easy to classify on this basis because they contain a mixture of elements some of which pertain to general education and others to vocational training. Because of widely differing views within and between countries about the relevance and the applicability of the distinction at third level the distinction is not maintained at third level except in a purely formal way. Persons holding a qualification which are coded as either '5', '6' or '7' on column 87 should be coded as '4' on column 86. As a convention for this survey "completion" always means sucessful completion normally accompanied by a specific qualification.

Persons who have not completed their studies, (i.e., persons who are code '5' in column 13 and code '6' in columns 69/70) should be coded on columns 86 and 87 according to the highest level, general and/or vocational, they have completed and should not be coded with a blank on either of these columns. Thus, for example, it would be expected that a person who was engaged in studying for an initial university degree and who had not had any vocational training prior to entering upon their current program of studies would be coded '3' on column 86 and '1' on column 87, unless the person already held a university degree in another field, in which case he/she would be coded as '4' on column 86 and '6' on column 87.

The national equivalences of each code used for these questions are set out in Annex V.

Col. 86 : Highest completed level of general education

This question is addressed to all persons 15 years or more, and provides information on the educational attainment of respondents.

The categories used in coding this item are broadly representative of those used in national publications of labour force data. However as countries differ widely in the way they categorise secondary education they have been expressed in standard international terminology as set out in ISCED (International Standard Classification of Education). Annex V shows details by country of the contents of each code.

Code 1 includes all persons who have not completed first stage of general second level education as defined in ISCED and as interpreted in national terminology.

Code 2 covers those persons who have completed ISCED 2 but have not completed the second stage of second level education as defined in ISCED and as interpreted in national terminology.

Code 3 covers those persons who have completed general second level education but have not completed a recognised third level program. In some countries as the proportion of each cohort which completes secondary education increases there may be post-secondary programs which are not vocational training in the sense of leading to a defined occupation but provide an enhancement of a person's general worth to the labour market at the same academic level as their secondary studies (e.g. acquiring familiarity with an additional language, or improving interview techniques). Completion of such programs should not be regarded as completing a program at third level. In general a program should be at least two years duration before it is classified as being at third level.

Code 4 is, as described above, used as an aggregate of those coded as either '5', '6' or '7' on column 87.

Code 5 is used for any other general education

Col. 87 : Highest completed level of further education or vocational training

This question is addressed to all persons aged 15 years or more: it provides information on the highest level of further education or vocational training completed by respondents.

It classifies respondents into three broad categories, those who have not completed any program of further education or vocational training (coded '1') those who have completed a recognised program at third level, usually by acquiring third level qualifications, (coded '5' or '6' or '7') and others (coded '2' or '3' or '4'). For those who have some vocational training, but cannot use any of the codes from '2' to '7', code '8' is used.

Countries differ greatly in the role assigned to an initial degree. Some countries have a short initial degree, which may be followed by an intermediate post-graduate degree, usually called a Master's degree, which may be followed by a post-graduate degree, a Doctor's degree. In other countries the initial degree is a longer degree and is regarded as a Master's degree. In addition professional degrees, such as medical degrees, which are typically longer than degrees in other fields, may be reported as equivalent to a basic degree in some countries and as equivalent to a postgraduate degree in other countries. For many years these differences have created difficulties in reporting statistics using ISCED and they remain to be resolved within the international community. In the Community Labour Force Survey the convention is to distinguish between code '6' and code '7' only in those countries where the distinction conveys useful information.

Situation one year before survey

Col. 88 : Situation with regard to activity one year before survey

The information collected through this question and those following in this section, is used to assess mobility of various types : between employment, unemployment and inactivity; of professional status; of economic activity; geographical mobility. Clearly such mobility measures, based upon the respondent's situation at two points in time, can only indicate at most one change in each case (for example, from unemployed to employed), whereas in fact several changes may have taken place over this period (for example, unemployed - employed - inactive - employed). Also, the International Labour Organisation definitions used elsewhere in the survey cannot be applied here, since not all the questions necessary can be asked (for example, availability for work, job search, etc.). The comparison must therefore be made on the basis of ILO definitions for the status in the reference week and a "main status" concept for the situation a year before the survey, as indicated below.

Code 1: Person was working

Persons with this code are considered as having been in employment a year before the survey.

Code 2: Person was seeking employment or was on lay-off

Persons with this code are considered as having been unemployed a year before the survey.

Code 4: Person was conscript on compulsory military or community service

Although conscripts on compulsory military or community service are excluded from the survey results, this code identifies persons who were conscripts a year before the survey. This is important in identifying labour force entrants.

Code 5: Other

Persons with this code or code '3' (pupil/student) are considered as having been inactive a year before the survey.

Cols. 90/91 : Economic activity of the establishment in which person worked one year before survey

The NACE codes in Annex II are derived from the Statistical Classification of Economic Activities (NACE Rev. 1).

Col. 92/93 : Country of residence one year before survey)

This should be provided according to the coding in Annex IV.

Cols. 94/95 : Region of residence one year before survey

This should be provided to the coding system in Annex I, which is based upon the Nomenclature of Territorial Units (NUTS).

Technical items relating to the interview

Col. 100/101 : Member State

This should be provided according to the coding in Annex IV.

Cols. 102/103 : Region of household

This should be provided to the coding system in Annex I, which is based upon the Nomenclature of Territorial Units (NUTS). The third and fourth digits of the NUTS code (that is, the level II regional code) should be provided.

Col. 104 : Degree of urbanisation

The concept of "urbanisation" has been introduced to indicate the character of the area where the respondent lives. Three types of area have been identified, as follows:

       densely-populated(Code 1)
       intermediate(Code 2)
       thinly-populated(Code 3).

An "area" consists of a group of contiguous "local areas" where a "local area" corresponds to the following entities in the respective Member States :

Belgique / Belgie	: Commune/Gemeente
Danmark	: Kommuner
Deutschland	: Gemeinde
Ellada	: Demos
España	: Municipio
France	: Commune
Ireland	: DED / ward
Italia	: Commune
Luxembourg	: Commune
Nederland	: Gemeente
Österreich	: Gemeinde
Portugal	: Concelhos
Suomi / Finland	: Kunnat
Sverige	: Kommune
United Kingdom	: Ward

The three types of area described above are defined as follows:

Code 1 : Densely-populated area

This is a contiguous set of local areas, each of which has a density superior to 500 inhabitants per square kilometre, where the total population for the set is at least 50,000 inhabitants.

Code 2 : Intermediate area

This is a contiguous set of local areas, not belonging to a densely-populated area, each of which has a density superior to 100 inhabitants per square kilometre, and either with a total population for the set of at least 50,000 inhabitants or adjacent to a densely-populated area.

Code 3 : Thinly-populated area

This is a contiguous set of local areas belonging neither to a densely-populated nor to an intermediate area.

It should be noted also that a set of local areas totalling less than 100 square kilometres, not reaching the required density, but entirely enclosed within a densely-populated or intermediate area, is to be considered to form part of that area. If it is enclosed within a densely-populated area and an intermediate area it is considered to form part of the intermediate area.

Cols. 114/119 : Weighting factor

Each person in the survey sample may be considered to be "representative" of a certain number of other persons not in the sample. The record for each responding individual is therefore assigned a weighting indicating how many persons are in this sense "represented" by this individual.

Col. 120 : Sub-sample in relation to the preceding survey

This information is included so that the common sub-sample between two consecutive surveys can be identified. Net changes between this year and the preceding one may thus be estimated.

Col. 121 : Sub-sample in relation to the following survey

As for Col. 120, this information is included so that the common sub-sample between two consecutive surveys can be identified. Net changes between this year and the following one may thus be estimated.

I

(Acts whose publication is obligatory)

COUNCIL REGULATION (EEC) No 3711/91
of 16 December 1991
on the organization of an annual labour force sample survey in the Community

THE COUNCIL OF THE EUROPEAN COMMUNITIES,

Having regard to the Treaty establishing the European Economic Community, and in particular Article 213 thereof,

Having regard to the draft Regulation submitted by the Commission,

Whereas, in order to carry out the tasks which are assigned to it by the Treaty, and in particular by Articles 2, 92, 117, 118, 122, 123 and 130d thereof, the Commission must be acquainted with the situation and developments in employment and unemployment;

Whereas the advent of the internal market increases the need for statistical information on the development of economic and social convergence so that comparisons may be made between Member States and regions in the Community;

Whereas the best method of ascertaining the level and structure of employment and unemployment consists in carrying out a harmonized and synchronized Community labour force sample survey, as has been done annually in the past,

HAS ADOPTED THIS REGULATION:

Article 1
Frequency of the survey

In the spring of each year, starting in 1992, the Statistical Office of the European Communities, hereinafter called 'Eurostat', shall conduct for the Commission a labour force sample survey in the Community, hereinafter referred to as 'survey'.

Article 2
Survey units

1. The survey shall be carried out in each Member State in a sample of households of persons residing in the territory of that State at the time of the survey.

Member States shall make every effort to prevent double counting of persons with more than one residence.

2. The information shall be collected for each member of the households included in the sample.

In cases where one member of the household provides information for other members, this shall be clearly indicated.

Article 3
Representativeness of the sample

1. The national statistical offices shall carry out the survey within the framework of national surveys and shall ensure that the sample of households referred to in Article 2 (1) corresponds to that usually adopted in the Member State in question, in such a way that the volume of the sample will be identical to that in the national survey.

2. In this context, to ensure a reliable foundation for comparative analysis at Community level, as well as at the level of the Member States and of specific regions, the sampling plan shall guarantee that for characteristics relating to 5 % of the population of working age the relative standard error at NUTS II level (or equivalent) does not exceed 8 %, assuming the design effect for the variable 'unemployment'.

Regions with less than 300 000 inhabitants shall be exempt from this requirement.

3. The national statistical offices shall take the necessary measures to ensure that at least a quarter of the survey units are taken from the preceding survey and that at least a quarter shall form part of a subsequent survey.

These two groups shall be identified by a code.

4. Member States shall provide Eurostat with whatever information is required for the organization and methodology of the survey and, in particular, shall indicate the criteria adopted for the design and extent of the sample.

Article 4

Survey characteristics

1. The survey shall cover the following characteristics:

(a) *demographic background, as follows:* relationship to reference person in the household, sex, year of birth, date of birth within the year, marital status, nationality, years of residence in this Member State, country of birth;

(b) *work status, as follows:* work status during the reference week, reason for not having worked at all though having a job;

(c) *employment characteristics of the first job, as follows:* professional status, economic activity of the local unit of the establishment, occupation, number of persons working at the local unit of the establishment, country of place of work, region of place of work, year in which the person started working for this employer or as a self-employed person, month in which the person started working for this employer or as a self-employed person, full-time/part-time distinction, permanency of the job, total duration of temporary job or work contract, number of hours usually worked, number of hours actually worked, main reason for hours actually worked being different from the person's usual hours, shiftwork, evening work, night work, Saturday work, Sunday work, working at home, looking for another job and reasons for doing so;

(d) *information about second jobs, as follows:* existence of more than one job or business, professional status, economic activity of the local unit of the establishment, occupation, number of hours actually worked, regularity of the second job;

(e) *previous work experience of persons not in employment, as follows:* previous experience of employment, year in which person last worked, month in which person last worked, main reason for leaving last job or business, professional status in the last job, economic activity of the local unit of the establishment in which person last worked, occupation in last job;

(f) *search for employment, as follows:* seeking employment for persons without employment during the reference week, type of employment sought, duration of search for work, main method used during past four weeks to find a job, date when person last had contact with public employment office to find work, willingness to work, as felt by persons who are not seeking employment, availability to start working within next two weeks, situation immediately before person started to seek employment (or was waiting for new job to start), registration at a public employment office;

(g) *situation of inactive persons, as follows:* situation of person who neither has a job nor is looking for one;

(h) *education and training, as follows:* education and training received during previous four weeks, purpose of the training being received during previous four weeks, total length of training, usual number of hours' training per week, highest completed level of general education, highest completed level of further education or vocational training;

(i) *situation one year before survey, as follows:* situation with regard to activity, professional status, economic activity of local unit of establishment in which person was working, country of residence, region of residence;

(j) *technical items relating to the interview, as follows:* year of survey, reference week, Member State, region, degree of urbanization, serial number of household, type of household, type of institution, nature of participation in the survey, weighting factor, sub-sample in relation to the preceding survey, sub-sample in relation to the next survey.

2. A codification document listing the characteristics of the survey, as indicated in paragraph 1, shall be drawn up and published by Eurostat after consulting the Committee on the Statistical Programmes of the European Communities set up by Decision 89/382/EEC, Euratom (¹), in accordance with the procedure laid down in Article 8 of this Regulation.

Article 5

Conduct of the survey

1. The national statistical offices shall conduct the survey on the basis of the codification document as described in Article 4 (2).

They shall ensure that the questions are in a logical sequence as regards their content and phrased in such a way as to guarantee, in collaboration with Eurostat, the maximum degree of comparability between the Member States.

2. Member States shall endeavour to ensure that the information requested is provided truthfully and in its entirety within the periods specified.

The national statistical offices may make it compulsory to reply to the survey.

Article 6

Transmission and publication

1. Within nine months of the end of the survey in the field, the national statistical offices shall forward to Eurostat the results of the survey, duly checked, for each person questioned without indication of name or address.

(¹) OJ No L 181, 28. 6. 1989, p. 47.

2. Eurostat shall be responsible for the processing, analysis and dissemination of the results of the survey.

The national statistical offices may, in consultation with Eurostat, publish the respective results of the survey.

Article 7

Statistical confidentiality

1. Items of information relating to individuals provided in the context of the survey may be used for statistical purposes only.

They may not be used for fiscal or other purposes and may not be communicated to third parties.

2. The confidential handling of data transmitted to Eurostat shall be governed by Council Regulation (Euratom, EEC) No 1588/90 of 11 June 1990 on the transmission of data subject to statistical confidentiality to the Statistical Office of the European Communities ([1]).

Article 8

Advisory committee

1. The Commission shall be assisted by a committee of an advisory nature composed of two representatives from each Member State and chaired by the representative of the Commission.

2. The representative of the Commission shall submit to the committee a draft of the measures to be taken.

The committee shall deliver its opinion on the draft within a time limit which the chairman may lay down according to the urgency of the matter, if necessary by taking a vote.

3. The opinion shall be recorded in the minutes; in addition, each Member State shall have the right to ask to have its position recorded in the minutes.

4. The Commission shall take the utmost account of the opinion delivered by the committee. It shall inform the committee of the manner in which its opinion has been taken into account.

Article 9

Entry into force

This Regulation shall enter into force on the day following its publication in the *Official Journal of the European Communities*.

This Regulation shall be binding in its entirety and directly applicable in all Member States.

Done at Brussels, 16 December 1991.

For the Council
The President
H. VAN DEN BROEK

([1]) OJ No L 151, 15. 6. 1990, p. 1.

Bibliography

Main publications of national survey results / addresses of National Institutes

Belgique/België
Enquête par sondage sur les forces de travail
Steekproefenquête naar de beroepsbevolking
INS / NIS, 44 rue de Louvain, 1000 Bruxelles - tel 32/2 5486211

Danmark
Arbejdsstyrkeundersøgelsen, Statistiske efterretninger
Danmarks Statistik, Sejrogade 11, 2100 Kobenhavn O - tel45 39173917

BR Deutschland
Bevölkerung und Erwerbstätigkeit, Fachserie 1, Reihe 4.1,
Statistisches Bundesamt, Gustav-Stresemann-Ring, 65189 Wiesbaden
tel 49 611751

Ellas
Labour force survey
National Statistical Service of Greece, 14-16 Lycourgou Street, Athens 101 66
tel 30/1 3248512

España
Encuesta de población activa
Principales resultados y resultados detallados (trimestral), Tablas anuales,
INE, Paseo de la Castellano 183, Madrid 28046 - tel 34/1 5839100

France
Enquête sur l'emploi - INSEE Première / INSEE Résultats
INSEE, 18, bd A. Pinard, 75675 Paris, cedex 14 - tel. 33/1 41175050

Ireland
Labour force survey
Central Statistics Office, Ardee Road, Dublin 6 - tel 353/1 6767531

Italia
Rilevazione trimestrale sulle forze di lavoro
Annuario statistico italiano
ISTAT, Via Cesare Balbo 16, 00100 Roma - tel 39/6 46731

Luxembourg
Bulletin du Statec
STATEC, 6 bd Royal, 2449 Luxembourg - tel 352 4781

Nederland
Enquête beroepsbevolking
CBS, Prinses Beatrixlaan 428, 2270 AZ Voorburg - tel 31/70 3373800

Österreich
Statistische Nachrichten
CSO, Hinter Zollamtsstrasse 2b, 1033 Vienna - tel 43/1 711280

Portugal
Inquérito ao emprego
INE, Av. Antonio José de Almeida 5, 1078 Lisboa CODEX - tel 351/1 8470050

Suomi / Finland
EU - Labour Force Survey
Statistics Finland, 00022 Helsinki - tel 358/0 17341

Sverige
The Swedish Labour Force Surveys
Statistics Sweden, Karla vägen 100, S115 81 Stockholm - tel 46/8 783 000

United Kingdom
Labour force survey quarterly bulletin
Office for National Statistics,
Great Georges Street, London SW1P 3AQ - tel 44/171 2703000

ES — Clasificación de las publicaciones de Eurostat

TEMA

0. Diversos (rosa)
1. Estadísticas generales (azul oscuro)
2. Economía y finanzas (violeta)
3. Población y condiciones sociales (amarillo)
4. Energía e industria (azul claro)
5. Agricultura, silvicultura y pesca (verde)
6. Comercio exterior (rojo)
7. Comercio, servicios y transportes (naranja)
8. Medio ambiente (turquesa)
9. Investigación y desarrollo (marrón)

SERIE

A. Anuarios y estadísticas anuales
B. Estadísticas coyunturales
C. Cuentas y encuestas
D. Estudios e investigación
E. Métodos
F. Estadísticas breves

GR — Ταξινόμηση των δημοσιεύσεων της Eurostat

ΘΕΜΑ

0. Διάφορα (ροζ)
1. Γενικές στατιστικές (βαθύ μπλε)
2. Οικονομία και δημοσιονομικά (βιολετί)
3. Πληθυσμός και κοινωνικές συνθήκες (κίτρινο)
4. Ενέργεια και βιομηχανία (μπλε)
5. Γεωργία, δάση και αλιεία (πράσινο)
6. Εξωτερικό εμπόριο (κόκκινο)
7. Εμπόριο, υπηρεσίες και μεταφορές (πορτοκαλί)
8. Περιβάλλον (τουρκουάζ)
9. Έρευνα και ανάπτυξη (καφέ)

ΣΕΙΡΑ

A. Επετηρίδες και ετήσιες στατιστικές
B. Συγκυριακές στατιστικές
C. Λογαριασμοί και έρευνες
D. Μελέτες και έρευνα
E. Μέθοδοι
F. Στατιστικές εν συντομία

IT — Classificazione delle pubblicazioni dell'Eurostat

TEMA

0. Diverse (rosa)
1. Statistiche generali (blu)
2. Economia e finanze (viola)
3. Popolazione e condizioni sociali (giallo)
4. Energia e industria (azzurro)
5. Agricoltura, foreste e pesca (verde)
6. Commercio estero (rosso)
7. Commercio, servizi e trasporti (arancione)
8. Ambiente (turchese)
9. Ricerca e sviluppo (marrone)

SERIE

A. Annuari e statistiche annuali
B. Statistiche sulla congiuntura
C. Conti e indagini
D. Studi e ricerche
E. Metodi
F. Statistiche in breve

FI — Eurostatin julkaisuluokitus

AIHE

0. Sekalaista (vaaleanpunainen)
1. Yleiset tilastot (yönsininen)
2. Talous ja rahoitus (violetti)
3. Väestö- ja sosiaalitilastot (keltainen)
4. Energia ja teollisuus (sininen)
5. Maa- ja metsätalous, kalastus (vihreä)
6. Ulkomaankauppa (punainen)
7. Kauppa, palvelut ja liikenne (oranssi)
8. Ympäristö (turkoosi)
9. Tutkimus ja kehitys (ruskea)

SARJA

A. Vuosikirjat ja vuositilastot
B. Suhdannetilastot
C. Laskennat ja kyselytutkimukset
D. Tutkimukset
E. Menetelmät
F. Tilastokatsaukset

DA — Klassifikation af Eurostats publikationer

EMNE

0. Diverse (rosa)
1. Almene statistikker (mørkeblå)
2. Økonomi og finanser (violet)
3. Befolkning og sociale forhold (gul)
4. Energi og industri (blå)
5. Landbrug, skovbrug og fiskeri (grøn)
6. Udenrigshandel (rød)
7. Handel, tjenesteydelser og transport (orange)
8. Miljø (turkis)
9. Forskning og udvikling (brun)

SERIE

A. Årbøger og årlige statistikker
B. Konjunkturstatistikker
C. Tællinger og rundspørger
D. Undersøgelser og forskning
E. Metoder
F. Statistikoversigter

EN — Classification of Eurostat publications

THEME

0. Miscellaneous (pink)
1. General statistics (midnight blue)
2. Economy and finance (violet)
3. Population and social conditions (yellow)
4. Energy and industry (blue)
5. Agriculture, forestry and fisheries (green)
6. External trade (red)
7. Distributive trades, services and transport (orange)
8. Environment (turquoise)
9. Research and development (brown)

SERIES

A. Yearbooks and yearly statistics
B. Short-term statistics
C. Accounts and surveys
D. Studies and research
E. Methods
F. Statistics in focus

NL — Classificatie van de publikaties van Eurostat

ONDERWERP

0. Diverse (roze)
1. Algemene statistiek (donkerblauw)
2. Economie en financiën (paars)
3. Bevolking en sociale voorwaarden (geel)
4. Energie en industrie (blauw)
5. Landbouw, bosbouw en visserij (groen)
6. Buitenlandse handel (rood)
7. Handel, diensten en vervoer (oranje)
8. Milieu (turkoois)
9. Onderzoek en ontwikkeling (bruin)

SERIE

A. Jaarboeken en jaarstatistieken
B. Conjunctuurstatistieken
C. Rekeningen en enquêtes
D. Studies en onderzoeken
E. Methoden
F. Statistieken in het kort

SV — Klassifikation av Eurostats publikationer

ÄMNE

0. Diverse (rosa)
1. Allmän statistik (mörkblå)
2. Ekonomi och finans (lila)
3. Befolkning och sociala förhållanden (gul)
4. Energi och industri (blå)
5. Jordbruk, skogsbruk och fiske (grön)
6. Utrikeshandel (röd)
7. Handel, tjänster och transport (orange)
8. Miljö (turkos)
9. Forskning och utveckling (brun)

SERIE

A. Årsböcker och årlig statistik
B. Konjunkturstatistik
C. Redogörelser och enkäter
D. Undersökningar och forskning
E. Metoder
F. Statistiköversikter

DE — Gliederung der Veröffentlichungen von Eurostat

THEMENKREIS

0. Verschiedenes (rosa)
1. Allgemeine Statistik (dunkelblau)
2. Wirtschaft und Finanzen (violett)
3. Bevölkerung und soziale Bedingungen (gelb)
4. Energie und Industrie (blau)
5. Land- und Forstwirtschaft, Fischerei (grün)
6. Außenhandel (rot)
7. Handel, Dienstleistungen und Verkehr (orange)
8. Umwelt (türkis)
9. Forschung und Entwicklung (braun)

REIHE

A. Jahrbücher und jährliche Statistiken
B. Konjunkturstatistiken
C. Konten und Erhebungen
D. Studien und Forschungsergebnisse
E. Methoden
F. Statistik kurzgefaßt

FR — Classification des publications d'Eurostat

THÈME

0. Divers (rose)
1. Statistiques générales (bleu nuit)
2. Économie et finances (violet)
3. Population et conditions sociales (jaune)
4. Énergie et industrie (bleu)
5. Agriculture, sylviculture et pêche (vert)
6. Commerce extérieur (rouge)
7. Commerce, services et transports (orange)
8. Environnement (turquoise)
9. Recherche et développement (brun)

SÉRIE

A. Annuaires et statistiques annuelles
B. Statistiques conjoncturelles
C. Comptes et enquêtes
D. Études et recherche
E. Méthodes
F. Statistiques en bref

PT — Classificação das publicações do Eurostat

TEMA

0. Diversos (rosa)
1. Estatísticas gerais (azul-escuro)
2. Economia e finanças (violeta)
3. População e condições sociais (amarelo)
4. Energia e indústria (azul)
5. Agricultura, silvicultura e pesca (verde)
6. Comércio externo (vermelho)
7. Comércio, serviços e transportes (laranja)
8. Ambiente (turquesa)
9. Investigação e desenvolvimento (castanho)

SÉRIE

A. Anuários e estatísticas anuais
B. Estatísticas conjunturais
C. Contas e inquéritos
D. Estudos e investigação
E. Métodos
F. Estatísticas breves

European Commission

The European Union labour force survey — Methods and definitions — 1996

Luxembourg: Office for Official Publications of the European Communities

1996 — 76 pp. — 21 x 29.7 cm

Theme 3: Population and social conditions (yellow)
Series E: Methods

ISBN 92-827-7240-3

Price (excluding VAT) in Luxembourg: ECU 7

The EU labour force survey was revised with effect from 1992.

This publication presents the contents of the survey from this date onwards, together with further documentation for the guidance of those involved in implementing the survey and of users of the data.

It replaces the previous edition, *Labour force survey — Methods and definitions, 1992* as the definitive description of the current survey.